with li

GINGER, WHERE'S YER DA?

For My Mother

GINGER, WHERE'S YER DA?

by
VIN McMULLEN

THE SPREDDEN PRESS
STOCKSFIELD AND LONDON 1996

PUBLISHED 1996 by
THE SPREDDEN PRESS
55 NOEL ROAD
LONDON N1 8HE

Printed and bound by
SMITH SETTLE
Ilkley Road, Otley
West Yorkshire LS21 3JP

CONTENTS

ACKNOWLEDGMENTS

It goes without saying that rarely, if ever, is a book the work of only one person, so it would be remiss of me not to say a sincere word of thanks to my family and friends for their encouragement.

Two of my friends and former colleagues deserve special mention. Peter Heneker is the very talented artist whose drawings have greatly enhanced the attraction of this modest work. Patricia Wilson typed, retyped and, with great patience, generosity and professionalism, contributed much to the production.

Vin McMullen,
October 1996

The publishers would like to thank the Local Studies Section of Newcastle City Library for their help in obtaining prints of photographs. 'Terrace in Wallsend' (p.35) and 'St Columba's church' (p.37) are printed by permission of Newcastle City Libraries and Arts and 'Evacuation of Newcastle children in September 1939' (p.48) and 'End-of-war street party' (p.76) by permission of Newcastle Chronicle and Journal Limited.

DA

'If you don't get them out of your head, they'll grow big – as big as horses when you're asleep. Then they'll carry you away and drop you in the river.'

The inside pages of the *Evening Chronicle* were spread across the table. With head bowed, I scanned the small meaningless print while Ma's heavy hand ploughed with a small tooth comb through the ginger jungle. The mere thought can still bring a tear to the eye and I can almost feel a red raw scalp – relieved only by the thrill of the kill. Dickies are what we called them, and as they fell to their fate and began scurrying across the Personal Column, heading for Miscellaneous Sales, we had to crack them with a turn of the thumbnail before they got to the Births and Deaths, for that was Ma's late night reading. It was also competition time.

'Ma, our David cracked that one twice.'

'No, I didn't.'

'Yes, you did.'

'A hundred didn'ts.'

'Anyway, I'm winning 7 – 5.'

'Quick, clear up. Here's Berna with her lad.'

Combs on the mantlepiece, bloodstained *Evening Chronicle* thrown on the fire. And me and our Dave giggled.

'Cocoa then bed, and say a prayer that your Da won't be drunk tonight.'

In old cast-off shirts too big we jumped and scrambled and dived into bed between sheets which, though clean, had been sewn and patched a hundred times. Snug and warm under a blanket and several old coats we said our prayers and laughed and kicked and punched and tickled until Kate came to join us.

'Let's play pork shops,' she said.

'Okay,' said David. 'I'm on ... letter P.'

'Pies?'

'No.'

'Pastie?'

'No.'

'Polony?'

'No. ... Will you give in?'

'No. ...'

'Oh, give in.'

'No. ... Oh, all right ... Peas Pudding.'

'That should have been P.P.'

'No, it shouldn't.'

'Ow! Stop kicking.'

These antics, interspersed with shouts for drinks of water, could last a long time, but somehow we arrived at a negotiated settlement to the many disputes and then we'd sink into unconsciousness overcome by sleep where we dreamt our dreams – and sometimes woke to a nightmare.

Bang! Bang! Bang!

'Open the bloody door!'

'Sh ... Sh! Bob, the bairns are asleep.'

Da was a soldier 1914-18 War

'Out my bloody way, woman!'

There followed scuffling and shouting, the crashing of plates and cups and then footsteps hurrying down the stairs.

'Da, sit down. I'll get your supper.'

Experience, even in those early years, had taught me to recognise that Berna's tone of voice was one of trying to humour a monster. Dave and I crept slowly downstairs, as we had several times before, frightened and speechless. As we peered through the kitchen door a terrifying scene overwhelmed us.

Ma held the tea towel to her face. Kate wrestled with her drunken Da, each struggling to gain possession of the poker, while Berna withdrew to the scullery with the kettle. I stood transfixed, paralysed, and then I rushed into the arms of my Ma.

'There, there. It's all right.'

But it wasn't all right. She knew that and I knew that and so did everybody else. Her eyes were swollen and she held a blood-soaked tea-towel. And now the soles of my feet poured with blood. I had run over broken crockery.

How I hated my no-good Da!

THE MOVE

Was it next day? Next week? Next month? I cannot say, but without a doubt I know that some short time later, when Da was out during the day, a horse and cart arrived at the door. It was obvious from the greeting and the friendly chatter that not only was the coalman known to the womenfolk in my family but that they had expected his arrival.

Like a military operation, they first of all started grabbing the brass candlesticks from the mantlepiece, then began rushing around putting all our precious bits and pieces into bags and sacks and boxes. Furniture was heaved as high as the rooftops, it seemed – sideboard, tables, chairs. Beds were broken into pieces and carried downstairs. The cart was piled high with my home, and Kate and Berna giggled, but it was no laughing matter for me. I did not know what had come over everybody. I was bewildered, terrified. I had never ever seen behind the sideboard and now I was looking at an empty house. I took in the deepest breath, filled my lungs to bursting and then let out the loudest roar of my life. Like lightning I was whisked from the chimney corner, to where I had retreated, and embraced by three pairs of feminine arms. My nose wiped with a pinny, I was buried in shoulder length hair and cotton blouses, my head was stroked and a soothing voice whispered, 'There, there, Vincey, we're going to live in another nice house.' But I did not want to move to another house. This was where I lived. This was my home. I had lived here since the beginning of the world. It was all I had ever known. It was familiar. I knew the faces in the wallpaper and every sound in the street. This must surely be the end of everything. The end of those happy gatherings in the evening around the street lamp with Harry and Alan Lee, Marjie Ewles, Joyce Venus and the Linsdell lads when we skipped and chanted:

'One, two, three O'Leary
I saw my Auntie Mary
Sitting on the lavatorie
Kissing Charlie Chaplin.'

The Move

It was the end, too, of our games of hide-and-seek, scrumping apples and knocky-door-neighbour. Goodbye to newts and frogs – and especially goodbye to Willy Venus's tortoise that I loved so well.

Those thoughts were locked in my head and heart. I did not know how to give them expression as I tearfully looked back and saw a small gathering of neighbours watching our departure from their front doors.

'It's going to be all right, Vincey, and your Da will never find us.' That was the only consoling thought as I sat behind the horse next to Mr Joseph Donnelly, Coal Merchant and Haulier.

We bumped and trundled and jostled over the cobbled roads of Wallsend and along the crowded terraces of back-to-back houses. The cart shook violently and we made several stops to pick up odds and ends that from time to time spilled onto the thoroughfare. Close-cropped lads with dirty faces and bare feet chased after us, stealing a ride by hanging on to the back of the cart, and teasing me with, 'Ginger, you're barmy.'

We clattered under the narrow railway arch, turned immediately right into Curzon Road and stopped outside an old semi-derelict building. Through the open door I saw a vast amount of old clothes, scrap metal, old baths, boilers and all kinds of junk. With a key Ma opened another door close by where a dark and narrow staircase led to the flat above. I was given the task of fetching water and holding the horse's head while volunteers arrived from who knows where to struggle up the stairs with our furniture. I was soon to discover that our new home was known locally as the 'rag shop' flat.

The womenfolk worked miracles transforming what was a cold inhospitable upstairs flat into something that resembled my home, but it was strange, especially that first night, to sleep in our bed in unfamiliar surroundings. It was also a new experience to be living in close proximity to a railway and in the dead of night to be jolted awake by the rattle and the whistle of trains which shook the house, sped through the bedroom door and out of the window into the black beyond. But, terrifying though that might be, it was still preferable to nights of terror of a previous existence.

The flat was small. We lived more or less on top of each other. The walls were damp and the ceiling bore clear evidence of a leaking roof.

Toilet and washing facilities were basic. To the rear of the house a flight of stone steps led to a tiny back yard where a lavatory that froze up every winter for several weeks, and a coal house, stood in one corner. A wooden tub, known as the poss-tub, and a wringer almost filled the remaining space. That was our laundry.

A batten door, with a Suffolk latch and a bolt, led to the narrow back lane that was always litter-strewn and dirty. Clothes lines were hung from wall to wall, and every Monday outside every home, for the full length of the lane, bed linen, shirts, blouses, underwear of all descriptions and sizes, were on show. So there was great pride in making certain that the whites were brilliant white and not a lighter shade of grey.

Winter and summer, I remember Ma struggling down the stairs with pans of boiling water. We all took a turn with the poss-stick – a kind of wooden stump with handlebars. We banged this primitive implement up and down in the tub to agitate the soapy water and thus produce clothes clean enough for public display in our back lane. Wash day was hard work in the summer, but in winter it was hell.

One evening every week the house was filled with steam. In the scullery every pan bubbled on the gas stove. Streams ran down the walls and on the misty window we drew happy faces with our fingers that quickly turned sad and then drowned in rivers of tears.

In the kitchen the black kettle sang on the hob in front of a blazing coal fire in which, amidst its embers and flames, we saw pictures. On the hearth stood the zinc bath the size of the table, though not so tall, with a handle on each end. Saturday night was bath night.

The sights, sounds and smells of the weekly event are as vivid now as if it were yesterday.

'Kate, keep the bairn out of the way, the big pan's coming.'

'My turn first in the bath.'

'No, it's not. I'm first.'

'Well, don't piddle in the bath, young un.'

'Ma, why doesn't our Kate have a bath?'

'Because, Miss Connell says, girls have to have their bath after their brothers have gone to bed,' interrupted Kate.

We wallowed in that luxurious carbolic feeling of cleanliness.

As the days and weeks passed I grew to like my 'rag shop' home.

The fireside, with its fender, brass candlesticks and blackleaded stove, was the focal point around which we gathered in the winter evenings, listening to Ma's stories, learning to tell the time from the clock on the mantlepiece, and toasting bread on a long fork in front of the bright embers. The lower the temperature outside the brighter the fire burned and we roasted our legs till they were crimson and mottled while our backs, by contrast, taking the full force of the draught from ill-fitting doors and windows, were freezing cold. So we took turns to sit on the fender with our backs to the fire.

From time to time Dave would chant his tables or catechism and Kate, with a book on her lap, attempted homework for she was now at Grammar School. On those cold winter nights I recall how, after cocoa and toast, we undressed in front of the fire then made a dash for a cold bed in a freezing bedroom, clutching a hot-water bottle. With head under the cover to help raise the temperature we somehow drifted into sleep and often, in the morning, woke to ice patterns on the window, and sometimes to a wonderful surprise.

'Look, young un. Get up quick! Look! The snow is here.'

I flew to the window and to the most delightful scene. The dirty street and back lanes and backyards, the rooftops, the chimneys were all transformed. No rubbish, no litter to offend the eye and the railway had ground to a halt. The white world outside was enchanting. There were no horses or carts or vans or lorries – nothing on the road but a thick white carpet. The postman alone disturbed the virgin snow with silent footsteps.

While the womenfolk slept Dave and I dressed hastily and raced to the door. Within seconds I was throwing snowballs wildly but within minutes I was frozen stiff and the joy turned to pain. The pain in my fingers and toes became intense. I ran indoors but the hearth seemed uninviting. The cosy glow of last night's fire had vanished. Only cold grey ash filled the grate. There was no comfort, no relief anywhere. I shivered and simpered and returned to bed, buried myself in blankets and coats till I heard the familiar metallic sound of the grate being cleared, and the clinking of pots and pans in the kitchen, which told me that very soon all would be well with my world. Within minutes my feet were on the fender, my face glowing before the fire, and my hands were clutching a bowl of porridge.

Ginger and Dave

Indeed, all was well with my world, or should I say that all seemed well with my world at that moment? I had one parent, who was as good as two, but she was not, and could not be, two. In those days it was very much a world in which every child had a Ma and a Da – except where one or other or, rarer still, where both had died. To me it seemed that the only socially acceptable explanation for not having a Da, was that he had died. So I repeated the lie time and time again whenever I was asked the dreaded question, 'Ginger where's your Da?'

But in those days everyone in the neighbourhood knew each other by name. They knew each other's business, too. The skeleton in my cupboard was common knowledge, but that did not deter me from keeping up the pretence. 'My Da died when I was a baby, so I don't know anything about him.'

I was ashamed of my broken home background. The wound had gone deep. I felt inferior and was almost incapable of even mentioning my Da to anyone for more than fifty years.

Looking back, I can now appreciate the kindness of neighbours, for it was a world where sharing was second nature, and the extended family also provided the security and solidarity without which we would have been poor indeed. Sitting on the fender that winter's morning long ago I felt deep down that my world was safe and secure in spite of all its problems and in spite of winter too which, in contrast to modern times, forced entry into every home and dominated our lives.

Of course we remember the good times and winter was sometimes fun, but all too often it was the enemy. The icy blasts which rattled the windows and whistled down the chimney also raised goose-pimples, nipped our ears and nose when we took our turn to negotiate, in pitch blackness, our way through the scullery and down the back stairs for a shovel of coal. But these things were child's play compared to the daily grind of the world's tenderest, toughest and most wonderful woman – my Ma.

MA

Ma was tiny – a mere five feet – and slim. She was also a bundle of energy and on those fierce arctic mornings, while her children were still breakfasting, Ma was off to work to earn a few shillings to support the family. Unless the snow was too deep a bus took her two miles to the cemetery where her main tasks were to clean the superintendent's office and the chapel. If the buses were not running she walked. In those dark winter mornings the virgin snow came over the tops of her Wellington boots and, often in blizzard conditions, she trudged to her daily toil with feet cold and wet.

When I reached the age of nine years I became a newspaper lad to help with the family budget and so, along with David and in solidarity with Ma, I shared the punishment of those bitter winter mornings. My round at one point converged with Ma's route to the cemetery and I can see her now crossing Holy Cross bridge battling with the wicked wind that would cut you in half. Wrapped in several layers under a tight-fitting coat she looked tubby. A woollen scarf protected her head, face and neck from the icy blasts of the north wind and old socks covered her gloved hands.

Ma's hands were a sight to behold. They were small, purple and swollen with chilblains. Her podgy fingers were split with winter keens. Her palms were coarse as sandpaper, and one of the fireside treats was to have your back rubbed with Ma's rough hands. Sensuality indeed!

By noon Ma's work at the cemetery was finished and she returned home, shopping on the way, for there was dinner to prepare for her family and also for her father who, although well past his eightieth birthday, had been working in Swan and Hunter's Shipyard since his retirement from the pit. For many years Granda would not move in with us. He insisted on 'keeping my own fireside'. All the adult opinion of the extended family seemed to concur that this was a wise decision but for Ma it meant a journey of about a mile each evening. Her whole life seemed to be one of toil, cooking, sewing, mending or

Ma

washing, and even while we sat around the fire her thimble and needle were in constant use. But sometimes fatigue won and she would simply fall asleep in her armchair by the fire.

How well I recall one evening I was lying on the hearth watching Ma's chin sink low on to her chest and her eyes close. I never liked that. Ma had to be there awake and alert to all my demands so I shook her knee.

'Ma, did you have a Da?'

'Yes, your Granda is my Da'.

'Does Granda get drunk?.'

'No, he's a very good Da'.

'Did you have a Ma?'

'Yes, Grandma is my Ma.'

And so the conversation continued till I acquired some understanding of my roots. Aunts and uncles fell into their places among my jumbled thoughts of family and extended family.

Ma was one of twelve children born to Jimmy and Catherine Rosanna McGuire. Jimmy's father, my great-grandfather, came to this country from Ireland during the potato famine and, while George Stephenson busied himself inventing a locomotive, my great-grandfather worked with pit ponies in the mines of Northumberland and Durham. His son, Jimmy, followed him into the mines when he was only nine years of age. Granda therefore never went to school and it was always a matter of great interest and amusement to his numerous grandchildren that he could neither read nor write.

GRANDA AND GRANDMA

Though Jimmy McGuire was illiterate, he was by no means simple, except perhaps in the sense of being uncomplicated and unsophisticated. But the virtue of simplicity was the hallmark of his life and lifestyle and, to my impressionable mind, Granda seemed to ooze peace, patience, contentment and wisdom. He looked solid and sturdy and, even though he stood a mere five-feet-two inches in his hob-nailed boots, Granda walked tall. He was every inch a proud working man of his time. His snow-white hair and full moustache could give him an angelic appearance – especially when his lined face was scrubbed clean and pink after his bath. But there was always a twinkle in the eye and a mouth waiting to smile.

On Sunday he wore his best cap, blue serge suit – always with a flower in the lapel – and a white shirt and tie. His Sunday boots were highly polished. Granda was a toff. At other times baggy trousers and open-necked shirt with no collar or tie was the order of the day. And there was always a cloth cap to cover his bald pate.

Granda's allotment garden, only a few yards from his frugal home in a colliery row, was his retreat, where he breathed clean air, worked his vegetable patch and sat beside the rain barrel and reflected. In earlier times, when the harsh reality of the Rising Sun Colliery was his daily experience, this was a place of therapy, a blessed plot indeed. Away for a few hours from the pitch blackness, the deafening noise and the back-breaking toil of the pit,

Granda

Granda became a steward of creation. He loved the soil. He loved, too, his show leeks. But most of all he loved daylight.

'Vincey, when I was your age you know what day I liked best? Sunday – that was when I saw daylight. You see, for weeks on end I went down to the pit in the dark and when I came up it was dark. I lived for Sundays. After Mass I had my breakfast and I walked for miles up the wagonway and along the hedgerows. Sometimes in the rain; sometimes in the snow; sometimes in the sunshine. It didn't matter. I was in daylight and breathing fresh air. Six days of hell, one day of heaven. That's the way it was for me Vincey lad, so make sure you work hard at school.'

Keeping the Sabbath day holy had a special meaning for young Jimmy McGuire. That was when he went to heaven for the day. The rest of his young life consisted of breathing in dust, standing – sometimes lying – in water, and straining every muscle cutting coal or filling trucks in an atmosphere of deafening noise, curses and profanities. The Granda I knew enjoyed his beer too, but that had not always been the case. One day Ma told me an interesting story of Granda that contrasted sharply with my experience of a drunken Da.

In the early years of his married life, when he had fathered several children (with more to follow), Granda took a day off and 'went on the beer'. As luck would have it, the parish priest called on his pastoral visit and was informed by Grandma that 'himself' was not at the pit but most likely in the pub.

Now Jimmy McGuire's voice may not have been the most tuneful but, with the help of several pints of ale, it was certainly the most powerful in all the colliery houses. The lyrics of 'My Irish Jaunting Car' could be heard, it was said, from the High Street, a distance of four hundred yards. That fateful day his Irish parish priest was witness to this remarkable feat but was not amused. He waited till Jimmy crossed the threshold and there in front of his anxious wife blasted him. 'How dare you take time off work to drink with all these children to support!' He raised his walking stick high and brought it down sharply across Jimmy's buttocks. The story goes on to say that Jimmy leant over the table saying, 'I think I deserve another one.' The parish priest obliged. What is apparently certain is that, after sleeping it off and sobering up, Granda later that evening knocked on the presbytery door and penitently asked his parish priest if he could sign the pledge.

According to Ma's story, Granda threw a party in great style at the wedding of each of his twelve children. Weddings in those days were very much a community affair and all of the colliery row joined in the celebrations. The beer flowed freely and the only sober man at the end of the day was the barman Jimmy McGuire who, in spite of his sobriety, took little persuasion to sing at least two or three songs from his extensive repertoire. The story continues that there was a notable exception to these wedding celebrations – Uncle Phil's. He was the youngest and last to marry.

It is said that in all the colliery houses for many years that party was considered to be the standard by which all other celebrations were judged. The beer flowed in rivers and this time Jimmy McGuire was as drunk as a lord, singing 'My Irish Jaunting Car', 'Dada's Baby Boy' and a hundred other classics before sliding under the table at or around midnight. His pledge after more than twenty years of iron discipline was smashed to smithereens, but as far as I know Grandma did not send for the parish priest.

Thereafter Granda enjoyed a drink on a regular basis but never over-indulged. Nevertheless, a friend and workmate who was a Methodist and total abstainer was overheard one day to give Granda some advice.

'Jimmy, it's a slow poison.'

'That's alreet,' said Granda. 'I'm in nee hurry.'

Grandma, on the other hand, was by no means an extrovert, but was well known and loved in all the colliery houses community, and I soon learned that if I wanted to be well received and accepted by adults far and wide I merely slipped into the conversation that Mrs McGuire was my Grandma.

My most vivid memory of Grandma was, in fact, the day that she died. I was engaged in a game of street football when word filtered through that Mrs McGuire had just died. Along with my cousin Jimmy Durkin, I abandoned the game and we nervously presented ourselves at the front door. 'Can we come in to see Grandma?'

We were ushered in to a packed bedroom where aunts and uncles knelt around the bed praying the rosary. Tears flowed freely. I felt a strange mixture of curiosity, fear and embarrassment. We were the only children present and I felt that we had trespassed into the adult world. What were they thinking of me, and would Ma be pleased that I had arrived on the scene, unwashed and with tousled hair? I looked at my hands. They were caked with mud and I thought everyone present would disapprove. The praying seemed to last forever and when eventually it came to an end everyone stood up and began speaking in a whisper.

'Come here, Vincey, and see your Grandma. She looks different.' She did too. She was not like Grandma. She was young, with no lines on her face.

'She looks different,' I said. 'Yes,' said Ma gently as she stroked my hair and buttoned my shirt. 'Your Grandma's happy now, because she's in Heaven.'

THE McGUIRES

'Ginger, how many cousins have you got?'

That was a fair question I could not answer. They were innumerable. Ma had six sisters and four brothers. They all married and subsequently produced large families. I well remember when I started school that an army of cousins was the best insurance against playground bullies. First and foremost was Jimmy Durkin, the sixth of seven children born to Aunty Evelyn. Jimmy and his four older brothers were each, in their day, saddled with the nickname of 'Duck' (a corruption of Durkin). This was none too popular with Aunty Evelyn and the lads themselves, on reaching a certain age, objected strongly to it – so much so, that a mere slip of the tongue might result in a fat eye. 'Duck' became Jimmy to me on a memorable occasion when, with my head tucked underneath his right arm, in a headlock, and his left hand tugging at my hair, he dragged me from the High Street, the full length of Station Road to the colliery houses, impressing on me that family solidarity included respect for Christian names. However, I still remained 'Ginger' to him, and everyone else for that matter.

Jimmy was my best friend. Father Rice, the Irish curate, referred to us as 'the inseperable pair'. We kicked a ball, swam, roller-skated, threw snowballs, sledged, fought, fell out of

Ma with first grandchild

18

friendship and made up before sundown. We collected cigarette dumps and re-cycled the tobacco by rolling our own. We were entrepreneurs in the firewood business, and for thruppence we would shovel a load of coal from the back lane into anybody's coalhouse. And all this before I reached the age of ten. We shared almost everything – even our birthday, July 12! Orangemen's Day meant little to us but, from the smiles and comments of adults we gathered it was not a fitting day for Catholics to be born. But that was all a joke. In our neighbourhood the only incident that I can remember was Grandma being called 'Virgin Mary Face' by a Protestant neighbour because she was sporting shamrock on St Patrick's Day.

Jimmy Durkin was exactly one year older than me. He was a shade taller and stockier with black curly hair and pointed features. He had a gift for music, but without any hope of developing his talent. He played the piano by ear and had a beautiful singing voice. He was a good footballer, too.

Jimmy was named after his father, whom I held in great awe. Uncle Jimmy seemed huge to me and resembled Victor MacLaghlan, a film star of that time, who always played the role of the tough guy. Uncle Jimmy was a miner, but in his later years worked in a shipyard foundry. He was heavily built with bald head and a lined face. Hard manual labour was written into every crease and wrinkle. He returned home from work late almost every evening, looking as if he had crawled through a hundred chimneys.

The Durkin home was in Diamond Street, a narrow row of colliery houses with two rooms downstairs – one a living-room-cum-dining room, and the other a kitchen-cum-scullery, from which a staircase led to three bedrooms. This was Auntie Evelyn's domain. She was short and stout and, from morning till night, seemed to shuffle slowly in perpetual motion from sink to pantry to gas stove to dining table, and she sighed deeply as she tackled the stairs, preparing beds and meals for the shift workers in her large family. By way of diversion she would cope with the family wash, too. Just another of the unappreciated working-class heroines who had no idea that she was a saint.

I would often sit in the living-room, taking in all the sights and sounds of a busy and noisy household – the singing, the banter, the arguments. I also watched in amazement while Uncle Jimmy annihilated the most enormous dinner, washing it down with tea from a pint pot.

In every living-room of every home the focal point was the black leaded fireplace and range, in which the fire invariably burned brightly. In the Durkin household it seemed like a furnace. The concrete floor was covered with oilcloth, and a home-made clippy mat in front of the fender gave a touch of domestic charm. The furniture and furnishings were frugal with one exception – the piano, upon which stood a statue of 'The Whistling Boy'. This was an artefact that might have been won at a fairground, no great work of art, but with a certain attraction. It depicted an urchin with shirt, breeches, battered hat, and a dog at his bare feet. Uncle Jimmy was a man of few words, except at Sunday lunch time when several pints of beer loosened his tongue, and he would reminisce. One story from his childhood predominated, so much so that all the family could silently mouth the words, so well did they know the lines.

'My dog was called Plodger. And when I was paid tuppence for a day's work, I bought two buns, one for me and one for Plodger. I would put my hands in my pockets, my hat on the back of my head and I whistled down the street.'

Then everyone joined in chorus, 'Just like him on the piano – the Whistling Boy!'

There were other occasions when Jimmy and I sat in the corner and concentrated on being invisible, the most memorable of all being New Year's Eve. As the magic hour of midnight approached, among the first to arrive were Uncle Jimmy and Granda, wearing broad smiles and their Sunday suits. They alone sat at the table and were the first to sample the broth and ham sandwiches, which had been prepared and were presented by the womenfolk. As they supped and ate they managed to sing too. It was invariably sentiment by the bucketful. Uncle Jimmy sang 'Memories', while the tears flowed freely down Granda's cheeks. Meanwhile, in the corner, two little lads remained silent, choking back their giggles.

When the clock struck midnight everyone took to their feet, glasses were filled and 'Happy New Years' were repeated and repeated while kisses and cuddles were passed around the room. People from who knows where seemed to charge through the open door and the singing began: 'Should Auld Acquaintance', 'Just An Old Fashioned Lady', 'The Miners Dream Of Home', and many more. Then followed the party pieces, the first one given by the host himself, 'There Goes Patsy Fagan'. Everyone joined in the chorus while Uncle Jimmy did his dance with a pint glass in his hand and never spilt a drop. By now there was enough music and song and merriment for Jimmy and myself to relax. The party was in full swing and no way would we be sent to our beds before dawn. We were revellers, party-goers, and wasn't it exciting?

KATIE

Katie, who was Ma's eldest sister, was also the closest to her. She was certainly my favourite, and she baked the most delicious crusty loaves. I always associated Monday with washing day, Auntie Katie, fish-and-chips and wonderful bread.

It was always evening when she arrived, long after the poss-tub had been emptied and stood in the corner of the back yard till next week. The clothes had been wrung out by hand, put through the wringer and hung up to dry before a blazing fire. The table cloth was the first to be ironed and I would lay the table in eager anticipation of the feast to follow.

As she entered the kitchen, Auntie Katie would sigh, comment on the weather, ask how everybody was keeping and send me for fish-and-chips twice. 'Be sure to go to Mickey the Greeks. He's the best. And ask for plenty of batter.'

Since I was the youngest, and Dave, Kate and Berna were grown-up, I was the only one at home to share those blissful Monday evenings.

Auntie Katie was smaller and stouter than Ma and she had a face full of fascination for me. It was lined and wrinkled and resembled a walnut. She had no teeth and I was intrigued to watch how far her chin came up to meet her nose as she chewed her crusty bread and chips. She was dressed almost always in black, stockings, dress and coat. Her hat stayed on her head even at the table, and that was black, too, and shaped like a soup plate. Two lots of fish-and-chips were shared three ways, though I got more chips than fish which suited me well. I soon learnt that if I sat quietly during these soireés, and better still pretended to be reading, I could listen in to all the gossip – hair raising stuff! I learnt that Mary Jane What's-Her-Name was expecting, though I could not work out quite what she was expecting. I gathered that her mother, who was 'all swank', would not be too pleased because Mary Jane was not yet married. 'And wait for it. She's going to get married in white'. I knew all this was privileged information that I did not understand so I held my peace.

Auntie Katie's two great loves were her Church and the Labour Party, from which, she claimed, the logical conclusion was that membership of one must lead to membership of the other. Her weekly door-to-door collecting – pennies from the poor – was to help fund the election of a Labour Government. What a picture her face was when, in 1945, Clement Attlee formed his government after a landslide victory!

Auntie Katie had endured hard times, too. Deserted by a no-good husband, she too had brought up four children single-handed. She seemed to me the most gentle and compassionate of Ma's sisters. Significantly, perhaps, she was also the one who had suffered the most.

Life was not, for any of the McGuires, a bed of roses. Maggie, whom I never knew, emigrated to Australia with her husband and young family to seek a better life and on the day she landed her baby died. This was surely a heartache from which she never recovered and it was common knowledge in the family that she was homesick until her dying day – some fifty years later.

Auntie Mary Alice had one child of her own and another adopted. She had a faithful and sober husband, Arthur, so with a small family it may be thought that life was easier for her, but she too had her cross to carry. Early in her married life she lost her sight.

Her adopted child, Lena, was a character and I liked her immensely. There were other opinions, especially among the adult relations. Lena was very much older than me, and, in fact, had a daughter my age. She was large – larger than life – frequented pubs and drank beer with the men. She was blonde, a kind of Diana Dors with a Geordie accent, and was loud, too. Not to put too fine a point on it, she was regarded by some as common. But she fascinated me. Always cheerful and friendly and, though I called her Auntie Lena in deference to her being a grown-up, she talked to me on level terms and seemed to have a sympathy for my broken family background.

When Lena discovered in her adult life that she was adopted, she exploded with anger. She felt that she had been deceived all her life by those she trusted and that was not only Auntie Mary Alice and Uncle Arthur, but the whole of the McGuire clan. She raised Cain, and everybody received a piece of her mind in no uncertain terms, and in full volume, too. But it blew over and, thank God, she was always my friend.

One occasion, in particular, stands out in my memory when she was just the right person at the right time. During my evening paper round I was set upon by another lad of my own age. It turned out that I was more than a match for him and, when the tide turned against him and I held him firmly in a head lock, he screamed for his father. I had not realised that the duel was taking place at his own front door. His father came at me, newspapers were scattered and he brought his heavy hand across my face. At that moment Lena turned the corner. She shrieked, sprinted the twenty or so yards and leapt upon him. As she beat the living daylights out of him, her tongue never stopped and her voice grew louder with every blow. 'Don't you dare touch that lad! He hasn't got a father to run to. But, by God, he's got me.'

The miserable wretch was glad to beat a hasty retreat. Lena, my friend, was much more use to me in that situation than any of my uncles would have been.

NORAH

Auntie Norah was different. She was younger for a start; younger in looks and in outlook, and she and David, her good and sober husband, provided me with five cousins. The two nearest to me, Philip and Hilda, were my friends, and it was they who introduced me to the swimming baths.

How could my first visit to the Wallsend pool ever be forgotten? Fitted out in one of Hilda's 'cossies' underneath my short trousers and woollen jersey, it was with more than a tinge of excitement that I set out with my two cousins. Wallsend High Street never seemed longer as we hurried and prattled our way towards the grey building behind the Town Hall.

As we approached the entrance, the noise seemed like a distant roar. Inside, we paid our entrance fee at a small window and progressed through swing doors to the pool. The sights and sounds were nerve shattering. Never had I experienced such mayhem! It seemed like there were thousands of children of every age packed into this huge building running and shouting and pushing each other into the vast expanse of water. Big lads were jumping off stairs and platforms and splashing everyone within range. My image of children swimming in orderly fashion disappeared in an instant. In fact, the thoughts of swimming at all seemed to be beyond the realms of possibility so overcrowded was the pool.

As many as six children shared one cubicle. There were two long troughs known as footbaths where everyone was obliged to wash. Floating on the surface was a grey foamy scum, but since the water was hot some children sat in it to keep warm. Others shivered in the shallow end of the pool while the more robust and accomplished managed a few strokes.

Phil and Hilda were old hands. They knew their way around, where to go, what to do, and spoke with an air of authority. 'Take your clothes off behind the curtain. Wrap them inside your towel, and put them under the seat, and then come here and we'll teach you to swim.'

The enthusiasm had left me. If I never swam in my whole life, I wouldn't be bothered. But I could not admit that. After all, hadn't Auntie Norah fitted me up with a 'cossie' and hadn't she given me tuppence to get in? I just had to go along with it. I joined the shivering hordes in the shallow end, and the session seemed to last for hours. I went through the motions of one learning to swim, but the humiliation of being taught by a girl one year younger than me added to the torture.

'Did you enjoy the baths?' asked Auntie Norah as she made us a cup of cocoa. 'Yes, it was great', I said. 'I'm really looking forward to going again.'

Phil and I were sometimes pirates and other times Robin Hood and Little John. Like most big brothers he did not encourage his younger sister to tag along, but I secretly enjoyed Maid Marion's company. They were not the 'street football' kind of pals but rather 'bows and arrows and camping' companions. We spent happy hours making secret hideouts among the gorse bushes in the Burn Closes and plodged and sailed our home-made boats in the stream. Phil always showed a preference for adventure and the great outdoors.

The McGills were a happy, secure and well-turned-out family and, if Auntie Norah put on a few airs and graces, who could blame her? After all they did live in Laburnum Avenue, a cut above the colliery houses, and in a different world to our rag shop flat. They had electric light, books on shelves, indoor toilet and bathroom, and Veronica, the eldest daughter, had really excelled. She was the first of the Mcguire clan to become a professional person – a qualified teacher. We all basked in reflected glory.

Two memories of Auntie Norah give me a warm glow. The first was when, somehow or other, she got David and me an invitation to a Christmas party in the Presbyterian Church Hall. The eager anticipation and the event itself were overwhelmingly joyous. My big nine-year-old brother, holding my hand firmly and protectively in his, led me through the door to the amazing sight of streamers, lights and balloons and tables heaving with sandwiches, scones and cakes of every description. In the centre stood a huge Christmas tree. A million children screamed and giggled and whooped with excitement as they awaited the 'starting gun'. It took my breath away. I was overcome with a mixture of fear and delight and I gripped David's hand more tightly.

When the announcement to take a seat finally came there was an almighty rush and we were left behind. For a few moments it looked like there were no places left but a bossy woman announced in a loud voice that made me cringe, 'There's one place on this table, and another on that one'. We were separated. At first I felt shy and lost, but I could see David looking anxiously from his place across the hall. We waved and soon, along with all the others, fell upon the amazing confectionery. When Santa Claus came, once again I nearly missed out. I was too shy to go forward to receive my gift, but 'Mrs Bossy' came to my assistance once again and took me by the hand to Father Christmas. I received a train set – second-hand and in a slightly soiled and battered box, but it worked. That was, for many months, my pride and joy.

The second occasion carved on my memory concerning Auntie Norah's thoughtfulness was when she sent me a ticket for a review, which was to be performed in the Parochial Hall. St Columba's parish in Wallsend had a proud record for amateur dramatics, due mainly to the gifted producer, Albert Cutter, who worked his craft mainly with the Boys' Club. Albert was short, fat and came to a point at his feet which made him cone-shaped. He was a teacher in St Columba's Elementary School and all I can remember of this much-worshipped son of the parish was his fierce temper, and that he had his favourites among whose numbers I did not feature. But it cannot be denied his stage productions, whether drama, comedy or variety, were always of a high standard. Tickets at a tanner each were snapped up by the better-off families. So when this ticket arrived I was overjoyed. I put it on display next to the clock on the mantlepiece for all to see and every day, before and after school, I took it down and read it aloud.

The Columbans Present
EASTER PARADE
Parochial Hall
7.30 pm
Saturday April 12th   6d

The tickets were printed with a bulldog printing set on pink card. I gave it to my friends to read, passed it round the table at mealtimes, and stood it against the sauce bottle so that I could read it for the thousandth time. The wait seemed endless but eventually I was there on 12 April (by coincidence, Ma's birthday), before the doors opened, to present a very grubby, dog-eared, sauce-stained, barely recognisable ticket, and took my seat in the front row.

The bright lights, the costumes and scenery captivated me. Lads that I knew danced and sang, and acted comedy sketches. I was captivated and stage-struck by my first experience of live theatre, but I was always much too shy to do anything about it.

For her kindness, Auntie Norah deserved the consolation of a happy and successful family. Nevertheless, she, too, suffered a broken heart. Philip started rock climbing in his teens and almost every weekend he took to the hills with his friends. In those days no homes boasted the luxury of a telephone, so it was not too rare an occurrence for a policeman to knock on Auntie Norah's door on a Sunday to inform her that Philip had missed the last bus and would not be home till next day. One Sunday evening the policeman's familiar knock brought Auntie Norah to the door saying, 'I know, he's not coming home tonight.'

'No, Mrs McGill, he's not coming home.'

A fall of rock somewhere in the Cheviot hills struck him about the head, crushing his skull and killing him outright.

WINNIE

Like all the McGuires, Winnie was short in stature, a mere five feet, and in her middle years she was also very stout. David and I amused ourselves with the old chestnuts such as, 'Auntie Winnie is as tall lying down as she is standing up'. I am sure that that was not the reason I received a clip around the ear when I was only five but, whatever it was that provoked such a chastisement, I have no wish to remember. Suffice to say, I kept a healthy distance from Auntie Winnie for some years to come.

Later, I realised that there was another side to her. Though her life had not been without sorrow, she was a jolly soul, especially at family celebrations when, at the drop of a hat, she would hold forth with her party piece, 'Two Irish Eyes'.

Wilf, her husband, died early in their married life leaving her with three daughters and a son. Her son, however, while still a baby, died shortly after his father, and her eldest child, also named Winifred, died at fourteen years of age.

Auntie Winnie and her two girls, Kathleen and Norah, were soon to become part of a much bigger family, for she married again. Ted Monkhouse, a widower with four children, moved into her home. The family increased even further with the birth of two sons, Donald and David.

I visited Auntie Winnie in her nursing-home when she was in her ninety- first year. Of course she had no idea who I was, but the mention of certain names of people and places produced a response, sometimes muddled, sometimes humorous and always lengthy as she mixed up her school days with middle age, the Durkins with the McMullens, and both families with the McGills. I tested her with the old songs. This time her memory was faultless. She started with her own party-piece, 'Two Irish Eyes', and then progressed through everyone else's party-piece too.

Of course, the geriatric residents were not unmoved by this unexpected entertainment, and in turn it inspired more spontaneity in song and dance routines. Before taking my leave of Auntie Winnie I exchanged some friendly banter and, when I leaned forward to take her hand and give her a kiss, would you believe it, she gave me a clip around the ear!

THE UNCLES

Ma often reminded me that I was named after her baby brother who died in infancy. 'Vincey, you have your own special saint in heaven.'

There were four more brothers but I did not have as much contact with them as I did with the aunts. Joe and John, I did not know at all, since they had moved away before I was born. Joe went to Kent and John 'disappeared' somewhere in South Africa.

Hughie was the one to hold centre stage at family parties. 'For my first song ... and then I will follow with an encore.' He talked like a tough guy and reminded me of James Cagney but always with the greatest of good humour. He was something of a role model to me. He lived in Benton Way with his wife, Jane, and their two daughters, Norah and Eileen. Norah was severely handicapped from birth and greatly loved by the entire McGuire clan.

Uncle Phil's wedding to Auntie Peggy. Granda and Grandma are on Uncle Phil's right

Uncle Phil was the youngest of all Ma's family. He was not a coal miner but a time-served engineer who married a school-teacher, Peggy Malia. They had a son named after his father and two daughters, Margaret and Pauline.

John was the uncle who interested me most, even though I had never met him. Family conversations revealed some information, but there were so many unasked as well as unanswered questions. As children we seemed to know that there was something about Uncle John that was not for our ears, so a whole area of his life was shrouded in mystery. What did filter through, however, was that the McGuires generally were proud of John. But was there also some shame and embarrassment?

During the 1914-18 war Uncle John was a soldier. He became a commissioned officer and had an honourable record serving with the British army in France. He was therefore not only the local lad made good, but also something of a local hero. I remember overhearing, or more likely eavesdropping on, an adult conversation when I picked up that Uncle John had got his 'Colliery Manager's Ticket' before joining up in Kitchener's army.

Related to the mystery of Uncle John, I came to realise, was Ma's closest friend, Auntie Annie, who lived in Benwell, the West End of Newcastle. It was a trolley bus and a tram ride from Wallsend, about one hour's journey, and something of an adventure to make the trip with Ma and the rest of the family. Auntie Annie had three grown-up sons who had endless patience with David and me. They introduced us to jigsaw puzzles and taught us simple card games, and Auntie Annie oozed kindness. Her scones and apple pie were all right, too!

As I grew older I became more and more aware of the relationship with the Aunt who was not Ma's sister, and my three cousins, and the missing Uncle John. But, for some reason, I did not probe to satisfy my curiosity until one Sunday when, in conversation with Granda over lunch, I shared with him my ambition to travel the world.

'One day,' I said, 'I'll go to South Africa and track down Uncle John.'

'Would you like to find Uncle John?'

'Yes, of course I would. Wouldn't you?'

'No.'

'Why?'

There was a long dramatic pause and the tears began to flow. And then he blurted out, 'Because I would kill the bugger.'

'No, Granda!'

After a long pause and more tears he added, 'He left your Auntie Annie to bring up those three lads alone. He was supposed to be going to South Africa to manage a gold mine and when he'd settled in and found a home he was to send for Auntie Annie and the lads. He never did. I tried to trace him, but nobody found him. I did find out that he was with a woman on the boat. That's all I know. I never thought I'd have a waster for a son. Yes, I'd kill the bugger.'

Four generations: Granda, Uncle John, his son (my cousin, John) and Great-Granda McGuire who came to England from Ireland during the potato famine

WALLSEND

Wallsend was a busy working-class town in those days. Its hub was the High Street which was its shopping centre and much more. It was the meeting place and gossip exchange for every age group, a hive of activity and bustle from morning till night. Within a few hundred yards there were five picture houses and many more pubs. Every kind of shop imaginable had its place on the golden mile.

At the centre of the metropolis another main road intersected with the High Street. This was Station Road running north-south and the main access to Swan and Hunter's shipyard where most of the town's menfolk earned their living. Of course there were more streets – hundreds of them – mostly paved with cobblestones, flanked with terrace houses and with the 'corner shop' at the end of every block.

Inside, these houses were mostly, though not all, spic-and-span where individuality and creativity were very much the affairs of women. Patterned wallpaper, home-made clippy mats, brass candlesticks, features in every household, might suggest conformity, but this was not so. Crocheted chair covers and embroidered table cloths and cushions provided scope for rich variety and colour while pictures and religious artefacts said much about the taste and faith of the family.

Externally every house was more or less a 'look-alike' of identical architecture with little opportunity for self expression – even the doorsteps were made to conform. The Saturday morning ritual which accounted for this brought the women to their knees at every front door. Wearing pinnies and headscarves, first they swept and then they washed and scrubbed their entrances. After this, they applied the 'donkey stone'. This was a kind of cross between soap and sandstone and, like the rouge on the cheeks of the women themselves, it was the doorstep's cosmetic. When it dried, all was smooth and bright and yellow.

Inside, maybe the sink was full of unwashed dishes, sauce and milk bottles still on the table at mid-morning, and beds unmade. But not many neighbours need know. The front doorstep, however – that was

Terrace in Wallsend

different! It was a public matter after all and there was always the moral pressure to 'do the step'.

There was a lot of pride in those communities and in the back-to-back terraces lived thousands of highly-skilled craftsmen, engineers, pattern makers, metal workers, joiners, electricians, draughtsmen and tool-makers, proud working-men.

Without the influence, support and friendship of a father at home,

I longed for the day when I would be introduced to the adult world through employment. That would mean going down the pit, working in the shipyard, or in one of the ancillary factories along the banks of the River Tyne.

The Rising Sun Colliery was situated more than a mile to the north, but the rows of colliery houses were much nearer the town centre. Coal miners and shipyard workers lived in close proximity and were thus one community. The West End, by contrast, was rather select – some might say toffee-nosed. It was where the professional and business people lived, and was called Walkerville. I remember thinking, how awful it must be to live there with no children playing football or rounders or cricket in the streets! And wasn't it quiet?

During my pre-school years, as I played out of doors in the virtually traffic-free streets, I could hear in the far distance what I can only describe as a rumble and occasional roar. I never quite knew what it was. It was part of the world that I accepted. Some days it rained, other days the sun shone, and sometimes it was just grey. But always the incessant noise. A few years later I discovered at close quarters that the distant rumble and roar was in fact the ear splitting sound of huge metal plates being cut, drilled and riveted in the process of building gigantic liners, cargo-boats and warships.

Those were days of full employment, and in my early years I stood amazed at the large numbers of men, dressed in boiler suits or bib and brace, who roamed the High Street during their lunch hour eating pies, sandwiches and fish-and-chips from newspapers while noisily exchanging banter with their friends on the other side of the road.

And there in the middle of the crossroads stood the local idiot, known to all the town's children as 'daft John'. John, a burly strong man in his forties, assumed responsibility for directing the town's traffic after the manner of the local bobby on point duty, though without any system and in the most hazardous fashion.

'How are you the day, John?' shouted the children as they passed by on their return to school after lunch break.

'How are you the day?' answered John.

'What time is it?' John would lift his left sleeve where no watch graced his wrist, but would look in a serious manner and reply, 'Quarter-to-one.'

36

St. Columba's Church: the 'tin cathedral'

It was always a quarter-to-one. The policeman standing close by beamed genially and it was smiles all around.

Wallsend was essentially a very friendly town, but if anyone went 'too far' in the baiting of John then he was certainly living dangerously. It was not the policeman he needed to fear but any one of the larger-than-life housewives who might be passing by. They all seemed to have a maternal instinct for poor John and could easily be angered by schoolboy antics and the indifference of grown men. It was not unknown, therefore, for an outraged woman to swing her shopping bag wildly and send a group of young lads running away in all directions. John would carry on his point duty as if nothing had happened.

St Columba's church was made of corrugated sheet metal and was sometimes nicknamed 'the tin cathedral'. Situated by the side of the railway on Carville Road, it was something of a landmark for train passengers travelling between Newcastle and the coast. Though externally the 'tin cathedral' could not boast any architectural merit, internally it had warmth and exuded a devotional atmosphere. Candles always burned in front of statues of the Blessed Virgin, the Sacred Heart and Saint Joseph, and it seemed that flowers in abundance always adorned the altar. Women from the parish called to 'pay a visit' on their way to and from the shops, and school-children during their dinner hour would drop in to join the devout women who knelt in prayer before the Lady Altar and the other shrines.

In spite of this being a holy place, or indeed because of it, children were not unknown to take a fit of giggles. Infectious laughter might even erupt throughout the entire child congregation. On other occasions the children would be treated to a little light entertainment. That is, if one or other of the two religious maniacs chanced to call. They were known to the young people as 'Kitty' and 'Holy Mick'.

Mick was small of stature, slim and had a pink complexion. His hair was cut and styled like a monk's tonsure, and it was snow white. Thus he looked the part – a stereotypical Holy Man. But he was mad. As soon as Mick crossed the church threshold something happened to him. Was it the sight of statues and candles or the smell of incense which lingered after Benediction that triggered this remarkable transformation? He would fall to his knees, beat his breast several times and then prostrate himself in the doorway. There he could remain for several minutes blocking the entrance and often barring the way for some pious old woman who became very impatient and even infuriated at his antics. When he at last stood up he would take two or three paces in the direction of the Lady Altar and then repeat the process. There were several more stops en route as he turned to bid time of day to statues. It could take Mick as much as half an hour to make his way from the church door to Our Lady. I was by no means alone among the children to find Holy Mick a source of amusement and fascination. We were, however, reminded by our teachers from time to time not to regard him as a saint, but rather as a sick man. This was just as well for, outside the environs of the church, Mick was said to have a 'wicked tongue'.

Kitty was probably in her seventies when, much to our delight, she attended the children's masses. Tall and slim, her well-groomed hair tied in a bun, she might have looked impressive, were it not that in other ways she was obviously eccentric. Dressed in a pinnie, a shawl around her shoulders, a shopping bag in one hand and a lighted candle in the other, Kitty would stand before the statue of Our Lady conversing aloud in a matter of fact way as she would with any of the women on the High Street. 'What a day! It's rained all night and all morning. Some of these bairns haven't got coats. And I've got a bad leg. Amen.'

Sometimes she would burst into singing a hymn, and it mattered not one jot if the priest and congregation were concentrating on the more solemn moments of the Mass. Kitty had her own agenda. At Communion she would present herself at the altar rails alongside the children and adopt the most dramatic pose with outstretched arms, eyes closed and her head turned heavenwards.

The most memorable occasion by far was when Kitty brought her goat to Mass. This was no mere distraction – it was a major disruption. To the children it was wonderful. But all too soon Kitty and her pet were persuaded and helped to leave. Nanny was hitched to a railing outside and Kitty returned to register a complaint to no less than the Blessed Virgin Mary herself! On Saturday Kitty would take her goat shopping and she found shopkeepers no more understanding.

Kitty and goat at Mass

Saturday afternoon was the time when the High Street was at its busiest for, as well as its being the occasion for weekend shopping and socialising, it was the children's tuppenny treat, the highlight of the week – the Saturday matinee. The Royal (better known as the Ranch) invariably had a full programme of Westerns. The Boro serialised *Flash Gordon*, the Queen's (the penny crush) played a mixed programme, The Tyne, *The Lone Ranger*. They all had a supporting programme of comedy shorts and cartoons.

I think I was about five years of age when I was first initiated into the Saturday matinee scene. It seemed to go with starting school. 'You're a big lad now, Vincey, so if you're good and go to school without a fuss, you'll be able to go the pictures on Saturday.' I shall never forget standing in line and then being pushed from behind as the queue surged forward and the old woman at the door struggled to collect everybody's tuppence. Inside, it was bedlam. It was futile to speak. If you wanted to communicate you must yell at the top of your voice adding to the mighty roar. A man wearing a peaked cap of authority and carrying a torch ran up and down the aisle screaming, 'Quiet, shut up, sit down. No you can't go the lavvie.'

There was a general stamping of feet and throwing of missiles when the lights went out and the cheering in unison almost raised the roof.

During the performance audience participation was taken for granted. Every villain was booed with great vigour and the goodies were cheered and applauded with uninhibited enthusiasm. It was also the occasion to buy sweets, monkey nuts and oranges.

Soon after war was declared, these commodities became scarce and later disappeared altogether. Some of us then took a turnip or a carrot and in the darkness of the picture-house we shared indiscriminately with our neighbours, passing along the row the half-eaten vegetables. It was prudent not to sit too close to a snotty nose!

For the rest of the weekend we relived these adventures and re-enacted in our games every detail that we had seen on the silver screen, interrupted only by two necessities, running messages for our parents and in my case delivering newspapers. Of course, there was also the requirement to go to church, which in those days not many people questioned.

SCHOOL DAYS

Adjacent to the church stood St Columba's school – a Victorian brick building of the 1870s. On the other side of the school was a large complex of offices, shops and stables. Collectively and individually these were known as 'the store' – that was the nickname by which the Co-operative Society was known locally. Almost everyone in Wallsend was a member of the store. It was where nearly all of the shopping and gossip occurred, and a place of daily pilgrimage. I was therefore familiar with the sights and sounds of St Columba's Infants' School, as viewed from the outside, long before that fateful day when I was taken by Ma to 'start school'. I did not want to go. My mind was in turmoil with a jumble of emotions but fear predominated. I was terrified.

Miss McElroy was tall and skinny as a lampost. On her head she wore a bonnet and around her shoulders a shawl. Her long dress reached to her buttoned 'winkle-picker' high-heeled boots, and her whole attire was black. Her pale face was scraggy and wrinkled. On the end of her pointed nose balanced a pair of tiny wire-framed spectacles. She was stooped and walked slowly. All the children knew that she was more than a hundred years old and that she lived in the school in a dark cupboard next to her headmistress's room. She spoke in a weak, squeaky, high-pitched voice, 'Quiet! Stop talking! Watch the signal!' She held up a wooden contraption that went 'click click'.

'I have a very big stick for boys and girls who don't stop talking. Are you ready? Hands joined, eyes closed. In the name of the Father and of the Son and of the Holy Ghost, Amen.' There followed Our Fathers, Hail Marys, Glory Be's, and we sang 'Angel So Holy' to our Guardian Angels.

Her every movement, every syllable, breathed piety – a devout woman who bored the pants off the children she loved dearly. She was a woman of her time, for though she was gentle by nature and, as far as I knew, would be quite incapable of inflicting violence on any child, nevertheless her daily exhortations to good behaviour were backed up by threats of corporal punishment, to be meted out with the mythical big stick that was allegedly locked in the dark cupboard where she lived.

Miss McElroy took all the new starters after prayers to her room where she told us that we must say our prayers every night before we went to sleep and every morning when we woke up. She gave us all a holy picture (I did not like mine as much as the other children's. It was of a man with a woman's face, with wings growing out of his shoulders, who she told me was Saint Michael the Archangel) and then she took us to our classroom to meet our teacher, Miss McHendry. As we left her room, I noticed a pool on the floor where Eileen McMenemy had been standing next to me, and I worried all day in case Miss McElroy thought that I had piddled on her floor. That, I thought, would surely be sufficient reason for the big stick to be brought forth from the dark cupboard.

The classroom seemed to be full of children even before the new starters arrived. Now it was packed and there were not enough chairs for everyone, so some of us sat on the floor beside a huge fireguard in front of the fire and next to the teacher's table. The windows were high in the walls so that all we could see was sky. We knew our mothers would be passing by to go to the store but we could not manage even a glimpse, though we could hear voices and the familiar sounds of the hustle and bustle outside. The clatter of the store milkmen and the store coalmen as they journeyed back and forward with their horses and carts were a major distraction, and I longed to be out there instead of all being gathered around the blackboard and Miss McHendry, like chickens around mother hen, chanting the alphabet phonetically.

There were cupboards with glass doors displaying toys, stuffed birds, a picture of the King and Queen, a statue of the Blessed Virgin Mary, a football and many other objects to distract us, and Miss McHendry constantly fought to keep my attention on shapes and squiggles on her blackboard which were of no interest to me. Meanwhile, I could hear the giant shire horses being led from their stables, the shouts of the men as they struggled to yoke up the magnificent creatures to their huge carts. Though I had witnessed the operation many times before, I longed to be out there away from the confines of the strange new world where old women's chief concerns in life seemed to be, at one time, to keep you still and quiet and, at other times, to have you chanting gibberish in chorus, as if a more fascinating world of horses and buses and trains and steam engines did not exist.

When the bell rang my heart lifted and I experienced a wonderful sense of relief. At last it was home time! But it was not! It was only playtime.

The schoolyard was a terrifying place – at least the boys' half was. Big lads, all in short trousers with legs like tree trunks, were running kicking a ball, chasing one another, wrestling and rolling in the dust. The noise was deafening. The new starters stayed together in a quiet corner, nearest to the girls' half where more civilised pursuits – dancing and skipping – were undertaken in a more organised and gentle manner. A high wall enclosed the playground and the wooden double gates were solid and locked securely. There was no escape, and playtime seemed to last for ever.

I ventured into the toilet block which separated the boys' from the girls' playground. The lavatory bowls were smaller than proper lavvies and stood in cubicles with no doors. I did not like them and when I looked inside I liked them even less. They were unflushed and filthy. Boys stood at the urinal and one big lad had climbed on to the wall and peed with amazing force and aim on the smaller boys below. I beat a hasty retreat and, in solidarity with Eileen McMenemy, wet my pants.

During the second half of the morning we copied squiggles and drew pictures on our slates, chanted our letters yet again, learned our catechism, said our prayers and, after what seemed to be an eternity, the bell rang for dinner time. Everyone went home. In the afternoon we had drill, we sang songs, modelled plasticine, stuck coloured sticky paper on cards, pulled hair and nipped bums until, at the end of the longest day in my life, we were released.

For the next eight-and-a-half years, until I left school at thirteen, I was the most reluctant of pupils. Truancy, however, was a rare event and did not feature at all until I was twelve but that is another story.

I was at my best in the evenings, at weekends and during school holidays. Living in an industrial town in close proximity to the countryside and educated in a Catholic school, I was a mixture of street urchin, rural delinquent and religious maniac. Pastimes and activities for me and my gang ranged from 'doing the natural' in Woolworths and the store, scrumping apples in suburban gardens, birds-nesting and collecting eggs, deliberately harassing the park-keeper to provoke a chase, camping out in makeshift tents, serving as altar boys at Mass, shuffling along the church bench on Saturday evenings to have our sins forgiven in Confession, and Thursday and Sunday evening attending church for rosary, sermon and Benediction. My morning and evening newspaper round, to supplement the family income, meant that I lived a full and busy life, but school and academic pursuits were clearly not one of my priorities.

After the Infant School years, I moved to the 'new school' – a large building where the juniors occupied the ground floor and the seniors the first floor. Miss Eccles was the headmistress of the junior school, and was in every way a marked contrast to the saintly and gentle Miss McElroy. In her day I suppose she was something of a modern Miss – elegantly dressed, always perfectly groomed, manicured fingernails and a hint of face make-up. She favoured the better-off, looked scornfully on poorer children, and a mere glance in my direction made me feel as if I had holes in my socks – I often had.

I lived in fear and dread of Thursday mornings when the whole school assembled for hymn practice. Along with several other lads I was stood to one side and told not to sing, 'Because you are grunters'.

Later the inquisition concerning Mass attendance took place and because I had not attended nine o'clock Sunday Mass – the Children's Mass – I was pulled by my hair to the front of the class and my face slapped. It was worse for those who had not been at all. But nevertheless I smarted under the deep sense of injustice, for as a paper lad I had attended the seven o'clock Mass. But to Miss Eccles that was of no consequence: 'Foolish mothers sending their boys out to deliver newspapers. Their shoe-leather must cost more than they earn.'

The public criticism of my Ma was unforgiveable. I hated the snob.

WAR DECLARED

In spite of the headmistress, the tone of the school was not all bad by any means. Kitty Campion, in Lower Juniors, and 'Granny' Connell, in Upper Juniors, were dedicated teachers with a high sense of vocation, but not, as I remember, with a noticeable sense of humour. Nevertheless, there was much homespun fun and entertainment in our lives – even in the darkest of days when the world was turned upside down.

Everyone knew that the war drums were rolling. It had been for some time the main topic of conversation in the shops and on the streets and wherever people congregated. We had seen on the newsreels the ranting of Hitler and jackbooted Nazis marching, and the build-up of tanks, guns, warships and aeroplanes. The whole atmosphere was threatening and an intense feeling of fear and foreboding filled the nation. I can vouch for the fact, however, that at least some young lads were just a little curious and even excited at what they thought might be an adventure, but on the whole they kept those thoughts to themselves because deep down they were frightened too.

It was a most memorable Sunday morning when Jimmy Durkin and I went for our usual walk after Mass. For some reason the war was not foremost on our minds and, no doubt, our thoughts and conversations focussed on football. They usually did. Everything seemed normal. The menfolk were walking in their navy blue serge suits, caps, white collars and ties in the direction of the pubs and clubs in the town centre, as they did every Sunday, while the women-folk, in flower-patterned pinnies, busied themselves in the kitchen, and the smell of Sunday roast started to emerge from open doors. My world oozed normality.

Jimmy and I stood at the bottom of Marshall's Bank contemplating Mr Middlemast's pear tree when suddenly doors opened, women ran into the streets shouting for their children. One old woman screamed at us, 'Get home quickly! War has been declared.'

Then appeared a small army of men wearing tin helmets and gas capes. They were blowing whistles, adding panic to confusion. We took to our heels. Jimmy disappeared in the direction of the colliery houses and I ran to Bernadette's new home. She had been married for twenty-four hours and her baby brother banged on her front door in a panic, screaming, 'The war's on. The Germans are coming.'

Her husband, Tommy, a man of good humour and endless patience, threw on some clothes and escorted me home. It was a good job, too, because over-zealous air-raid wardens had for some unknown reason sealed off all routes leading to the High Street. There was chaos beyond all anticipation as the menfolk poured out of the pubs and clubs, the womenfolk ran through the streets calling for their children, and children responded to the atmosphere by screaming uncontrollably.

Tommy negotiated my safe passage home where my anxious Ma looked relieved beyond measure to see me. We remained indoors for the rest of the day, with frequent glances out of the window expecting to see German aircraft and even paratroops darkening the sky.

But nothing happened. No aeroplanes, no guns – in fact it was just like peace. And that's the way it was for days and weeks ahead, except for one huge disruption and trauma – evacuation!

It was deemed necessary for all schoolchildren to be removed from industrial Tyneside – a likely target for German bombers. And the contingency plans that had, no doubt, been prepared for months were now put into effect. There was no school for the first few days of war and then we were all assembled with our mothers to hear of the arrangements for evacuation. Ma put her name forward as a helper, so we lived in hopes that she would accompany us, but that was not to be. Another younger woman was chosen and Ma was bitterly disappointed. David and I were devastated and we did not want to go, but persuasion and moral pressure were applied and we joined the long line of children at Wallsend Railway Station the following Monday.

Ma made us haversacks from hessian. These were stuffed with a change of clothes and for the first time in my life I had pyjamas. She hid a small toothcomb in David's pack: 'Don't let anybody see this. You'll be out in the countryside so comb your hair on the grass.'

'Do we need the *Evening Chronicle*?'

'No, as long as you get rid of the dickies you don't have to crack them.'

We had a label with our name and address pinned to our lapel and

Evacuation of Newcastle children in September 1939

in our pocket an addressed postcard to Ma to tell her where we were. No one had been told where we were going.

The train journey was high adventure. From the window we saw rivers and lakes, woods and hills. I thought that we were far away from civilisation and it seemed like we had travelled a hundred miles when eventually we stopped at Ashington Station. We transferred to a bus which took us to Lynemouth, a mining village by the sea in south-east Northumberland.

The assembly point was the village school where evacuees were assigned to waiting adults. It was, I suppose, a bit of a cattle market, but most of us were too apprehensive to make a fuss. One lad, however, did kick up a rumpus when he discovered that he was to be separated from his big sister, so much so that an on-the-spot conference reorganised matters more to his liking.

Dave and I went with 'call me Granny' Mrs Crawford. She was very much the stereotype Granny, in her sixties, small of stature, chubby with a ruddy complexion, grey hair tied in a bun and wearing a pinny. Hers was a home-sweet-home, spotless and bright. The coal fire burned in the centre of the highly polished blackleaded range and reflected in a hundred brasses and in the sideboard mirror. A beautifully patterned clippy mat adorned the floor. Sitting on a rocking chair in the chimney corner, smoking his pipe, was Mr Crawford – 'Granda'. He was a quiet man, always dressed casually in a collarless shirt, waistcoat, baggy trousers and slippers, who smiled contentment and nodded agreement to all his wife had to say. We could not have been more fortunate. It was, indeed, a happy, secure home.

Every day Granny gave us a ha'penny to buy our bottle of school milk according to the regulations. When she discovered that we bought toffee lollipops instead, far from chastising us, she increased our allowance to a penny.

'Now, here's a ha'penny for your milk and another ha'penny for your lollipop. Promise you'll drink your milk?'

Granda Crawford chuckled in the chimney corner.

'What was he laughing at?' I asked David as we set out for school.

'I don't know, but I think he likes us.'

We responded to her kindness and dutifully bought our bottle of milk every day.

Evacuation turned out to be something of a paradise for the evacuees who became known as the 'townies' to the good people of Lynemouth. The local school buildings could not accommodate the increased child population, so we were required to attend half days only – mornings one week, afternoons the next. This gave plenty of scope for exploration, mischief and adventure. Every day we combed the beach and rock pools which, in those days, were pollution free. Winkles, crabs, starfish and other unidentifiable sea creatures were our delight and fascination and were taken prisoner in jam jars. We made rafts with driftwood which never proved to be seaworthy but invariably fell apart within minutes of their launch. We lit fires and roasted spuds taken from nearby fields.

In the evenings and weekends we explored the countryside, made tree houses in the woods, chased pit ponies in the dene, and trapped rabbits with home-made snares. We romped in meadows and jumped on haystacks, pulling them to pieces without a thought for the hard work we were undoing. Occasionally the farmer or the local bobby caught a 'townie' red-handed, but there was amazing sympathy for the 'poor bairns', separated from their parents by the circumstances of war, and not a single misdemeanour was punished. The 'poor bairns' exploited this sympathy in full measure.

It was not surprising that after a few months of phony war, with no reports of air raids on Tyneside, some of the evacuees started drifting home. In many cases the host community did not discourage them. After spending Christmas at home most of the 'townies' did not return. As for David and me, we did go back after Christmas, but in early January we too returned to the bosom of our family.

SENIOR SCHOOL

On our return to Wallsend we very quickly picked up where we had left off but there were some changes. We moved house. Ma's ambition to move to the other side of the railway was realised. The distance was a matter of a few hundred yards, but psychologically it was a hundred miles. Ma felt that it was much more 'respectable' to live on the other side of the tracks, and the house we moved to was an upstairs flat directly opposite St Columba's Church on Carville Road.

This was not far for Kate to walk on the arm of Granda when, at eighteen years of age, she married Jimmy Burton. They moved into the front room, for no houses were available for newly-weds during the war. Jimmy became my big brother – bigger and much older than David. He took me hiking and cycling and camping and we planned even greater adventures when the awful war would at last come to an end.

The downstairs flat was occupied by a delightful couple of octogenarians, Mr and Mrs Trevorrow, whose whole demeanour breathed peace and tranquillity. I became their Saturday errand boy for fourpence. Theirs was a home-sweet-home too, and I loved the smell of pipe tobacco which had seeped into every crack and cranny and had been absorbed into the curtains and furnishings. We now had a rented wireless and so did all our neighbours. News bulletins of the war, commentaries and variety programmes became topics of conversation in queues which formed outside every food shop and everywhere else where people congregated. Even the school playground buzzed with excitement at the news of the shooting down of enemy aircraft, or the sinking of a German warship. We sometimes overlooked the casualties inflicted on our own forces. Our mind was set on the promised early victory. Morale-boosting songs became well known and sung by everyone and were now even part of the repertoire of our music lessons.

As time went by we came to realise that a quick victory was just a pipe dream. Air raids became a nightly experience and we spent hours crouching in the cupboard under the stairs with Mr and Mrs Trevorrow doing jigsaw puzzles and listening to the bangs and clatter of anti-aircraft gunfire emanating from warships on the River Tyne. And then the crump, crump, crump – a different sound that we learnt to identify as high explosive bombs falling on our town. It was often frightening, but there was one consolation: if the all-clear siren did not sound till after midnight we had the morning off school. We prayed that the German aircraft would fly over the River Tyne every night but drop no bombs and then be shot down at five-past-midnight.

The next morning, during our newspaper rounds, the paper lads got the first pickings of shrapnel and the remains of incendiary bombs that were often strewn across the town. In spite of all that, Tyneside suffered little damage compared to other industrial centres.

At school I graduated to the senior department upstairs where, for the first time, I had a man teacher, 'Sandy' McNulty. Sandy had a reputation for fairness and toughness, which really meant he hit everybody, without exception, at frequent intervals – in the religious lesson for not knowing the catechism, in the maths lesson for not knowing tables and in English for spelling mistakes, but most of all in the history lesson for not memorising history dates. The history lesson was a reign of terror which consisted of copying dates into a notebook, learning them, and then being tested. The end result was that frequently one might receive up to a dozen strokes of the thick leather strap. I shall never forget the intense pain when I first experienced the teaching method of this sadist.

But a few minutes' reflection prompts me not to be so judgmental. It is true that Sandy's regime was indeed oppressive – but not totally, and he did introduce us to English literature. He read and we followed, in our books, *Treasure Island, Kidnapped, Huckleberry Finn, David Copperfield* and *Prester John*. I was enthralled, not only at the stories but also at the skill of the narrator. That was Sandy's forte. And, if he did rule with an iron rod – well, that is the way it was. At that time the consensus in society seemed to be, 'It didn't do me any harm'. That was the rationàle of almost every adult in the nation. So Sandy was just a child of his time, a product of the same system that had been passed on through generations.

A small incident occurred in Sandy's class that might have been of such insignificance as not to be worthy of mention or even remembrance, but yet it has remained vivid in my memory and it shines like a bright star in my treasure trove of recollections.

Tom Hastie was promoted to Sandy's class, and was allocated a place next to me to share a double desk.

'Where do you live Tom?'

'Benton Way.'

'My Uncle Hughie lives in Benton Way.'

'I live with my Granny and Granda.'

'Why? Is your Da away in the war?'

'Yes.'

'And your Ma?'

'No, she lives with Granny and Granda as well.'

'What about yours? Is your Da away in the War?'

'Eh ... ye ... yes ... No, he's dead.'

'What did he die of?'

'I ... er ... I don't know ... But I have a Granda. He's eighty-four and still works in the shipyard.'

'What's his name?'

'Jimmy McGuire.'

'I've heard my Granda talk about Jimmy McGuire.'

'What's your Granda's name?'

'Mickey Glass.'

'Yes, my Granda knows him. They work beside each other.'

We opened our desk lids, with heads down pretending to be searching for a book as we choked with silent laughter, celebrating the feeling of solidarity and friendship within minutes of introducing ourselves. But there was something of far greater significance to follow.

'Ginger, you know I said that my Da was away in the war. Well he's not. He left my Ma and me. He was a gambler and not very good. Promise you won't tell anybody.'

The relief, the joy that filled my soul cannot be described. At last there was somebody else like me. I was not the only one in the world – not even in the school – with a no-good Da. And, moreover, I had a friend in whom I could confide. I shared everything with Tom and he with me. Our friendship developed and became deep and lasting.

We were Scouts together. We hiked and camped and cycled. We

dreamed dreams and fantasised about Grey Owl, a Red Indian brave who lived in wide open spaces and hunted wild animals. Grey Owl could live a sustained life-style in forests, was familiar with a thousand living creatures and could identify the tracks of all the animals. He was conversant with nature's wonderful works. We wanted to be like Grey Owl. That's what we would do when we grew up. We would go to Canada and live like Grey Owl or be backwoodsmen, or even lumberjacks, and wear check shirts and denim trousers. We would have bronze bodies, huge muscles and grow beards. When we returned to Wallsend for a holiday all the girls in the parish would be eating out of our hands, and we would spin a coin for Pauline Abbott.

The headmaster, Joe Nichols, was a kinder man, but unfortunately had suffered shell-shock during the 1914-18 war and, without warning, was capable of exploding into the most terrifying fit of temper. One safeguard, however, was that you always had warning of his approach. He carried a bunch of keys in his right hand and because of his condition his arm shook uncontrollably. Our headmaster was thus nicknamed Jingling Joe.

In spite of the strict regime, with a strong reliance on corporal punishment, the lads still challenged the system. We enjoyed adventure which in those days often meant mischief and misdemeanour.

One morning in spring, having finished my newspaper round, I took a short cut through Wallsend Park. The lake in those days, if not crystal clear, was at least clean and pollution free. Stickle-backs, minnows, newts and frogs abounded, and from the steep banks you could view the small island on which swans nested. On this particular morning I could see clearly a large white egg among the twigs and rushes.

Times without number the women in my life had appealed on behalf of our feathered friends and exhorted me not to steal their eggs. 'It's like someone stealing a baby from the pram. How do you think the mother feels?'

These exhortations were based on the supposition that boys have souls. That morning I felt a tingle, my pulse began to quicken and the challenge excited me. I could not wait to get to school to share the news and to discuss the strategy with trusted friends of a similar turn of mind.

Charlie Wales and Terry Campbell, nicknamed Sambo, were my chosen accomplices. 'There's at least one egg – perhaps two or three.'

At dusk, just before the park closed for the night, we arrived by the lakeside armed with crusts of bread. We hid in the bushes until we observed Tashy Blinkers, the parkie, set off to lock one of the gates. The lake was irregular in shape so we lured the swans to the bank furthermost from the island. It was Sambo's task to feed them bread, while Charlie and I, with shoes tied together by their laces and strung around our necks, set off wading, taking the shortest crossing. We pulled our short trousers high to our waists in an effort to keep them dry. Charlie was rather timid and dallied nervously a few yards behind. My heart beat fast – a mixture of excitement and nervousness overtook me. Then, just as I clambered up the retaining wall of the island, a whistle blew from the bank top, Sambo disappeared into the bushes, Charlie turned and beat a hasty retreat, and I decided to go for it. I raced across the island while whistles seemed to be blowing from every direction. There were two eggs and I lifted them both and fled. I slid down the retaining wall up to my shoulders, but I soon recovered and tried to run through two feet of water. My heart pounded faster and I eventually reached the bank and, hot on the heels of my pals, made for the last gate to be locked at night. To my relief it was still open, and as arranged I shot across the road into the valley where, in the long grass, we hid until the whole world around us was black dark and silent.

On our way home we hid the eggs in Charlie's allotment and composed a story of why we were late and how I came to be soaked to the skin.

The next morning as we assembled in the school playground for morning prayers we noticed a visitor talking to Jingling Joe. It was Tashy Blinkers. The headmaster addressed the assembly.

'After prayers, on your way to classes, you will walk in single file up to the Park Keeper and look into his eyes.' My stomach turned. I felt sick and trembled with fear. This was surely my 'come-uppance'. I could hear my mother saying, 'It's like stealing a baby'. Perhaps they would take me away and I would be locked up.

'Dear God, please don't let Tashy recognise me. Please, please, please! I won't ever commit another sin. I won't steal any more birds' eggs. I won't scrump apples. I promise. Just don't let Tashy recognise me. Hail Mary full of grace.'

The lines started to move and I braced myself for the worst. I walked forward, my pulse racing and my fists clenched tight. I looked Tashy in the eye and kept walking. I arrived in my class a nervous wreck, but soon regained composure. He had not recognised me. The power of the Hail Mary!

At playtime I boasted to all my mates of the swan's eggs hidden in Charlie Wales's allotment.

Kate with her baby feeding swans in Wallsend Park. 'Don't steal her eggs. It's like stealing a baby from its pram.'

FUNERALS AND WEDDINGS

Funerals were often joyful occasions – but only if the deceased were advanced in years. The death of a young person was quite another matter.

When Granda died at eighty-seven years of age in Ma's bed in our front room in Carville Road, I was very upset and, since I could not cope with my emotions, I took to walking the streets of Wallsend for an hour or so.

Aunts and uncles had gathered earlier on that Sunday afternoon when the bedside ritual of endless prayers began, and Jimmy McGuire sank into unconsciousness and eventually breathed his last at about six pm.

It seemed that his eyes were hardly closed before the kettle was put on to boil, and cups of tea, scones and apple tart were passed around. And though everyone still spoke in quiet tones there seemed to be an air of relief and the hushed atmosphere gradually gave way to one of normality. Within minutes more relatives, friends and neighbours started arriving. First they went into the bedroom to pay their respects to the corpse, say a brief prayer, and come to the kitchen for a cup of tea and hear every detail of the last hours of Granda. It was at that point that I took my leave. I needed to be alone with my thoughts and to say my own prayers and shed a tear or two.

On my return I found the house was full of people chattering and reminiscing. Stories of Jimmy Mcguire were told and retold. And there was laughter and an almost joyful atmosphere. It seemed like a celebration and this continued into the night.

The following day was quiet with only a few callers coming to pay their respects, but in the evening, when the Legion of Mary came to say the rosary around the coffin, installed in Ma's bedroom, there was a full house.

The funeral was impressive. The church was packed and many attended the graveside ceremony then returned to our house where tea and the customary ham sandwich and pastries were served to all-comers. In the evening the men went to the pub and returned for supper, and a party of sorts took place, for it was felt that in reverence to his memory a medley of Granda's songs should be sung. Thus an hour or two of singing, laughter and tears rounded off the funeral-cum-wake of Jimmy McGuire.

Brian Brownlee was only eight years of age when, during playtime, he trespassed indoors, presumably to take a drink of water at a handbasin in the cloakroom. I can still see Bill Skivington's face as he came flying into the school-yard announcing, 'There's a lad dead in there.'

Of course, we all laughed. But Bill's eyes bulged, his cheeks had lost their ruddy complexion and he shook from head to foot. Then he lost his voice. He was in deep shock, and some of us close to him realised something was amiss. We were never allowed indoors during playtime, but a delegation, throwing caution to the wind, raced into the school and hammered on the staffroom door. Within seconds there was confusion as garbled information quickly spread and within minutes there was a stunned silence in the playground as the entire school population came to realise from the behaviour of their teachers that indeed something very serious had happened. Eventually we were assembled to say prayers for a boy who was seriously ill.

No one can be sure what happened, but conjecture has it that Brian, alone in the cloakroom, had somehow got his neck entangled in a roller towel, slipped off water pipes on which he was standing, and choked.

The whole town turned out to his funeral, and mothers lining the route along Wallsend High Street wept profusely as the hearse passed on its way to the cemetery.

Weddings were joyful occasions, but these had the complication of two sets of families coming together who might not know or even like each other; so, generally speaking, we enjoyed funerals more than weddings.

Altar boys, however, always enjoyed weddings, for there was a vested interest. Serving at a Nuptial Mass invariably brought a tip from the best man, so it was the most cost-effective pastime for a Saturday morning, with the possible exception of pumping the church organ. The choir loft was small, made to accommodate a dozen or so choristers in front of a large organ, at the side of which was a long wooden lever. To make music the organist required a man or two boys to work the bellows by pulling and pushing the lever up and down. It was not easy work and was known as 'pumping the organ'. The word 'pump' had also quite another meaning. It was an indelicate, though not the rudest term, for someone breaking wind.

On one auspicious occasion when a respected son and daughter of the parish were joined in Holy Matrimony, two less-respected twelve-year-old sons of the parish, Nick Roberts and Jimmy Quinn, were engaged to pump the organ, and the fee was a whole florin. That is, one shilling apiece! It was indeed big money. But, when they were recruited, little did Miss O'Neill, the organist, know that she had taken on a problem. Jimmy Quinn, it could be said, suffered from flatulence. His friends described his affliction more graphically, while Jimmy himself regarded it as a talent that he could produce sound and odour at will.

He practised his gift as a kind of cabaret spot for his friends' entertainment. Perhaps it could be said he had no sense of occasion for just as the bride arrived in church and the organist had struck a chord, Jimmy (voluntarily or involuntarily, who can say?) made his contribution. By the time the bride had reached half way down the aisle Nick Roberts began to feel the full effects and started to laugh quite heartily. Laughter, being infectious, was taken up by Jimmy Quinn. By now there was no strength in their arms – no power in their pulling and pushing. The organ started to groan for lack of air and Miss O'Neill leaned across, poked her head around the corner, and in a stage whisper said, 'Pump, boys, pump'.

That was it! They collapsed in a heap, laughing uncontrollably, while the organ died.

Needless to say, they were sacked on the spot. A sidesman came to the rescue and thereafter the wedding continued without a hitch.

'Pump, boys, pump!'

SEASONS AND FESTIVALS

The seasons and festivals, both secular and sacred, filled our lives with expectation, interest and excitement. Autumn was, for us, the season of scrumping apples and blackberrying. We looked forward to the joys of Guy Fawkes, with its bonfires, twopenny rockets, Jumping Jacks, Catherine Wheels and bangers. And then we counted the days to Christmas.

On the first day of December the paper lads, with varying degrees of artistic talent, produced their own greetings cards. On small rectangles of red manila, we drew holly leaves and berries and wrote little verses. Mine was always the same:

> My lot is a hard one people admit.
> And gladly I welcome a Christmas gift.
> So here's to wish you good Christmas cheer.
> And the best of all a prosperous New Year.
> *With the newsboy's compliments.*

With economy in mind we produced only one card each and this we handed to every customer in turn, asking for it back after they had read it. Of course, they got the message and, with a smile, most people dropped a thruppenny bit into the tin. If you were lucky, and you had called on the right day at the right time, you might have been given a tanner. Dave and I competed fiercely for who would raise the most in tips by Christmas Eve. Our boxes were hidden under the bed, and each night before we went to sleep, like two misers, we counted the spoils.

As Christmas drew nearer, paper decorations appeared through every window, sprigs of holly on front doors and small Christmas trees adorned sideboards. Shops were a fascination to the younger children who pressed their noses hard against the windows as they dreamed their dreams of Santa Claus, presents, and stockings filled with every imaginable delight.

Our carol-singing syndicate was Jimmy Durkin, the Flannery brothers and me. While other lads, who formed trios and quartets, played away serenading the middle class and better-off families, expecting rich pickings, we played the home patch, the colliery houses, and invariably more than doubled their takings. But we kept the secret to ourselves.

Excitement and eager anticipation for the festive season moved us always to try carol-singing too early – in the first week of December. Our enthusiasm at that time was rarely shared by adults, so we came to regard the expedition merely as a dress rehearsal for the big occasion – Christmas Eve, when we made an early start wrapped in hats, coats, mufflers and gloves, carrying a jam jar with a string handle and a candle inside. These home-made makeshift lanterns often presented a problem. Invariably, the heat of the candle caused the jar to crack and eventually to fall apart, so we took turns to light our lantern with the hope that we would still have at least one in working order at the end of the evening. It was not just to create atmosphere that we carried them – they were functional, too, for in the wartime blackout there were neither street lamps nor lights in the windows. It was pitch black – except for those cloudless, moonlit nights. The most memorable were the bright frosty variety when the ground sparkled like diamonds and our toes, fingers, nose and ears tingled. But in spite of the bitter cold we were happy to continue. Our excitement increased with every coin that was dropped into the kitty and, since I was the bagman, I struggled to keep a running total.

'The bag's getting heavy. I'll bet we've got a quid each already.'

As each front door opened the warm air stroked our faces and we heard and felt and smelt the joy and magic of Christmas that rushed to meet us. Parents brought their toddlers to the door, 'Say Happy Christmas to the carol-singers'.

The wide-eyed little ones repeated, 'Happy Christmas', and mothers, fathers, grandparents and older children smiled and chuckled and sometimes joined in the singing. At some front doors grandmas brought mince pies, while others treated us to mugs of cocoa.

Jimmy Durkin was the only one with any kind of singing voice so he was soloist, and was called upon to give a rendition of 'Silent Night' at nearly every house. The Flannery brothers led us all in 'Adeste

'Silent Night'

Fideles', while I, being unable to sing in tune, was encouraged to remain in the background *sotto voce*.

At around nine pm we were obliged to call it a day, for we were keeping the younger bairns out of their beds on this special night. The contents of the bag were then counted, we divided the proceeds and went home with light hearts and heavy pockets.

Ma had a pan of broth simmering on the hob.

'Here, this'll warm you up, you look frozen.'

'Hey Ma, I've got a lot of money. Look at this!'

I emptied my pockets on the table – ha'pennies, pennies, thruppenny bits, and tanners. There were even one or two bobs.

'My God, where have you been?'

'Carol-singing, Ma, it was great. I'm going to buy you another Christmas box when the shops open.'

Sitting in front of the fire with a bowl of broth, I was soon snug and warm and suddenly I felt all aglow even to the depths of my being. I was secure, comfortable and loved – and it was Christmas!

Christmas Day came and went. New stockings were stuffed with nuts, oranges and apples and were hung from the brass rod which was suspended from the mantelpiece. David and I feigned surprise at our presents that we had already discovered some weeks previously in a box on top of the wardrobe.

We survived Mass, avoided the hugs and kisses of fond aunts and enjoyed a breakfast of bacon, eggs and black puddings. Whatever the weather the warm glow stayed inside us as we shared the Christmas spirit with our friends.

Christmas dinner was just like Sunday's. Turkey was outside our experience, chicken an expensive luxury, so roast pork was our usual festive fare. But what made it distinctive was a drop of sherry, followed by a dash of beer in a tumbler full of lemonade. Christmas pudding, which followed, filled our bellies to capacity, and the bloated over-fed feeling became associated, especially, with Christmas afternoon – so did Ludo, Snakes and Ladders, and Draughts.

Tea-time was later than usual – it needed to be. Then Ma and the girls began once more to prepare a table that was a picture of conscious excess, heaving with savouries, fruit-cakes, jam tarts, apple pies and a host of other delights.

Blindman's Buff, Hide-and-Seek and guessing games kept us going until bedtime when, invariably, we fell into a deep sleep.

In the New Year we looked forward to the snow which arrived with unfailing predictability, and then a hundred children, with caps and coats and scarves, and boots and sledges, converged noisily on the banks of the Little Burn. Within minutes they were hurtling down the steep slope, shouting and whooping with delight.

When there was a particularly cold snap the park lake would freeze over and, while it had been known for someone to make an appearance wearing ice skates, it was mostly an occasion for hordes of children to slide on studded boots in all directions, creating a situation of noise and confusion as they bumped one another, skidded on their backsides and cracked their heads on the ice. Tears were shed and blood was spilt, but in the main it was a celebration of youthful exuberance.

Of course in February, as the gradual thaw crept upon us, the ice might give way to the weight of so many bodies and some would be thrown into the icy water, screaming with shock and the intense cold, while others stampeded for the bank where they convulsed with laughter as they watched their unfortunate friends clamber back on to the frozen surface which gave way further with every step. When, at last, they made the bank, how they shivered and cried as they ran home!

In every season even the smallest pleasures loomed large in our minds – especially if they had become institutionalised into annual events. After winter sports but before the daffodils we looked forward to Pancake Tuesday. We prattled for several days about how our Ma could throw them and we repeated far-fetched stories borrowed from the *Dandy* or *Beano* of pancakes sticking to the ceiling. Afterwards we exaggerated the number we had consumed.

'You should have seen our Ma throwing pancakes all night. I had six syrup and five with jam.'

The next day was Ash Wednesday when the whole school population assembled in church for nine o'clock Mass. At the homily spot Father Timothy O'Brien had a wonderful time reminding us of the only certainty in life – death!

'I know not where, when or how,' he bellowed. 'But one thing is certain. I will die. We shall all die.' For fifteen minutes of increasing

65

eloquence and uninhibited gesticulations, interspersed with dramatic pauses, he proceeded to terrify the life out of a captive audience of school children.

'Then that body that we pamper will rot in the grave to be eaten by worms. And our immortal soul will go before Almighty God in judgment.'

' "Come ye blessed", He will say, or perhaps', another dramatic pause, ' "Depart from Me, ye cursed, into Everlasting Fire" '.

To reinforce the message everyone advanced in single file to the altar rails to be blessed with ashes on the forehead by the parish priest or his curate. With each anointing, words were spoken in Latin. Later in our classrooms the message was repeated in English: 'Remember man that thou art dust and unto dust thou shalt return.'

Inclusive language in those days was not an issue, so the girls asked no questions about their mortality. Like the boys they concerned themselves only with the ashes to see who had the biggest splodge.

The less sensitive souls in the congregation and classroom day-dreamed, as they usually did, through the entire performance while others quaked in their boots at the thought of Hell for all eternity. Silently they begged forgiveness and promised God that, in reparation for the sins of twelve pancakes on the previous day, they would eat no sweets for the whole of Lent – even until Easter Sunday!

Lent came and went. We attended more Masses, paid more visits to church, made the Stations of the Cross, but in all probability ate as many sweets as ever – except, of course, on Good Friday, the Fast before the Feast.

On Easter Sunday we dressed in our best, wore something new and rolled our paste eggs down grassy banks in the park. In spite of adult disapproval some of us were known to walk behind the 'Sally Army' band (anywhere for a little apple!) as they celebrated the Feast of the Risen Lord. There were daffodils in abundance in gardens and allotments, and now, it seems, that in those far-off days the sun always shone at Easter. As spring changed to summer the days lengthened and street games and activities took over.

STREET GAMES

Kevin Flannery was the wizard on the wing. His ball control was exceptional, and in the tradition of the very best of wingers of our day, Stanley Matthews, he would 'sell the dummy', beat his man and take the ball to the corner flag, from where he would lob the perfect centre. The only difference was, that while Stanley Matthews played outside right for Stoke City and England, Kevin Flannery was outside left for Diamond Street Rovers.

Kevin's two older brothers, Tony and Jimmy, and his young brother, Peter, were also staunch members of the team. Jimmy Durkin, strong in tackle and with dogged determination never to concede a goal, never mind defeat, was the mainstay of defence at centre half. Charlie (Fatty) Sansome was the blustering full back, a bully who threatened and intimidated any of the opposition who had the temerity to stray too near our goal mouth. A number of guest players from neighbouring streets would be invited to make up the illustrious eleven. On the strength of Cousin Jim being the captain, I had a regular place on the team.

At one end of the colliery houses ran Harle Street which had a smooth and wide expanse of tarmacadam. This was our pitch for daily practice. It was also the scene of many a squabble, which not infrequently culminated in black eyes and bloody noses when we failed to reach a negotiated settlement to one of the many disputes. A referee was a luxury outside our experience. We would have ignored him anyway.

Wallsend could boast of other teams besides Diamond Street Rovers. St Luke's was the local amateur team whose home ground was close at hand. It was enclosed within high walls and fences and had a turnstile at the gate. An imposing stand could be seen from a distance but, once inside the ground, one could not but be impressed by the quality of the turf, the marking of the pitch and the nets which dressed the goal posts at each end.

On Saturday afternoons it was common practice to award ourselves free entry to home games by way of a spuggy's (sparrow's) ticket. We 'flew' over the wall. Mid-week, Diamond Street Rovers often granted themselves free access again and full use of the facilities. In fact it had been known for fixtures to be played there. On one memorable occasion the game came to an abrupt end when the main door opened and there stood the club secretary, Mr Middlemast (the one with the pear tree in Burn Avenue!). We scattered in all directions, scrambled over the fence, and disappeared – all except one. I had gone to retrieve my jacket from behind the goal and was caught by the wrist in the firm grip of Mr Middlemast.

'What's your name?'

'John Jones.'

'Where d'ya live?'

'17 Queen's Crescent.'

I blurted out those lies without a moment's hesitation. It was a new experience and, even though I was terrified at what might happen to me, there was a certain amount of pride at my prowess. I suppose I was subconsciously looking forward to the time when I would be boasting to all the lads how I had pulled the wool over the eyes of 'owld Middlemast'.

I can still feel that firm grip on my wrist as he marched me in the direction of Queen's Crescent. I panicked: 'I don't live in Queen's Crescent.'

'You don't, eh? Well, where d'ya live?'

'I'm not tellin ya.'

He continued in the direction of Queen's Crescent.

'How embarrassing,' I thought. 'If he takes me to 17 Queen's Crescent, what'll I say?'

'*What'll I do?*'

The frog-march continued. I was relieved when we walked past Queen's Crescent. But the relief was short-lived. 'I'm taking you to a better place than Queens Crescent.'

It dawned on me that we were going to the Police Station!

Sergeant Cairns was a man mountain with a purple face and ginger moustache, and a voice of thunder. There was no need to hold my wrist now. I was petrified – glued to the spot.

'What's your name?'

'Vincent McMullen,' I squeaked.

My voice was shaky and weak, my breathing irregular. I panted and shook from head to toe.

'Who was with you?'

'Jimmy Durkin.'

'Who else?'

'Jimmy Flannery, Kevin Flannery.'

I spilt the beans. No one was left out. No heroics – just plain fear and cowardice. And now the long walk to each of their homes with Sergeant Cairns walking three paces behind, catching up with me frequently to box one or other of my ears with his leather gloves.

The humiliation was intense. There I stood at the doorway of each of my friends' homes, in turn, while Sergeant Cairns gave a full account of our misdemeanours. The thoughts of the punishment that was to follow this preliminary ordeal flooded my mind. But did I spot a wink of the eye and a hint of a smile on the face of Sergeant Cairns? All I can say is that, when we convened next day, not one of the gang reported any severe chastisement from parents and furthermore the lads did not take me to task for grassing.

There were other games and diversions. British Bulldogs was a noisy robust game of rough-and-tumble which favoured the big and hefty and was very popular with the Fatty Sansomes of this world. As for me I was skinny, slightly undersized and not fast enough to keep out of trouble. So it was not one of my favourites. Rounders, I liked. It was also very popular with the girls for they could play on level terms. The only equipment needed was a chair leg and a tennis ball, and to excel all you needed was a good eye.

'Keep your eye on the ball, young un', our Dave would shout as we threw a ball to each other for hours on end. I thus became a proficient catcher, and I could also whack the ball over backyard walls scoring a rounder with almost every pitch. On more than one occasion the ball not only flew over the wall but also crashed through a scullery window. The sound of breaking glass put both teams to flight with individuals lying low for an hour or so in various coalhouses and lavvies. When we emerged, perhaps inspired by the recent experience, we might organise a game of hide-and-seek. The girls liked this one too and sometimes the game was known to change its objectives and even degenerate into a blatant version of 'catchy kissy'.

A story circulated among the children in the locality, and believed by the younger ones, was that some years ago a skeleton had been found in a cupboard in a derelict house and in the coat pocket was a medal inscribed, '1931 WALLSEND HIDE AND SEEK CHAMPION'.

During the war, brick air-raid shelters, with reinforced concrete roofs and no windows, were constructed in many streets. They were put to many uses as well as the obvious, that of a safe haven against the attacks of the Luftwaffe. For the children they served as a den where, in candlelight, all kinds of dramas and concerts were performed, stories told and dreams dreamed. In secret, away from the interference of adults, we exchanged information about the facts of life. The more knowledgeable stated the case bluntly and emphatically and the rest of us listened in wrapt attention. But some of us were not convinced. I for one just could not believe that my Ma would indulge in what we knew to be sinful, dirty practices. In fact some of us would say, 'No girls would do that, would they? Would they?'

And then it was off to Confession. 'Forgive me Father for I have sinned. I have committed adultery.'

'Tell me what you did.'

'Well, Father, we sat in the air-raid shelter saying and listening to dirty things.'

'That was not adultery. You have committed sins of impurity by thought and word. You must not go into that air-raid shelter ever again. It is a dangerous occasion of sin. And you must not keep bad company. For your penance say five Our Fathers and five Hail Marys. Say a prayer for me.'

It felt great to be in a State of Grace. I could die now and not be sent to Hell for ever.

Those air-raid shelters had other uses. When the spirit of adventure and mischief welled in our breasts we could play an improved version of 'knocky-door-neighbour'. A short skipping-rope would easily reach the knobs on the front doors of two adjacent houses. We would tie them together, give a loud knock and then retire behind the shelter from where we would peep, helpless with laughter as the two neighbours contested with each other to open their front doors.

Of course that was an expensive diversion, for invariably we lost a skipping-rope – no one dared to retrieve it in case of capture. Another version was just as entertaining. After dark we would tie black thread to the door knockers and again retire behind the shelter. We would then give the thread a tug, thus producing a sharp rap on the door. Quickly we would let out some slack so the door could be opened and we would watch the astonished neighbour as he peered to the right and to the left, looking for the invisible caller. As soon as the door closed, we repeated the exercise with great glee, and of course the evening's entertainment often ended with the thrill of a chase.

Most of our games and diversions took place in or around the colliery houses, but not all. Wallsend Park was renowned for its bowling greens and flower beds. But there was also a labyrinth of narrow paths which meandered up hill and down dale through woodland and by streams and lake. It was truly a place of beauty as well as our adventure playground.

The hills were a godsend for all manner of home-made wheeled vehicles – bogies, we called them. But at one time we acquired another much more sophisticated means of transport which could accommodate the whole gang. It was a long basket chair.

Jim and John Stark were twins. At about the age of eleven Jim contracted tuberculosis in the hip, and the treatment was total rest. To facilitate this he was encased in plaster-of-Paris from foot to midriff. He was also given a long, full-length bath-chair, so that his brother and friends could take him for gentle walks.

As many as eight of us were known to climb on this wonderful bogie, with John standing on the rear axle and controlling the steering mechanism. As we sped down the steepest hill we whooped and shouted and screamed with delight, no one enjoying the thrill more than Jim, our disabled chum. Old men and women remonstrated and waved walking sticks menacingly, but we were oblivious to danger. We were having fun and no doubt eight guardian angels were working overtime to prevent a disaster. Sometimes the chariot overturned and spilled its contents into the bushes and flower-beds and as far as I can remember there was never any blood spilt. No doubt there would have been had Mrs Stark discovered why we were so keen to take her beloved Jim for a gentle stroll through the park.

A SURPRISE VISITOR

In our little world news travelled fast. During the war years rumours travelled even faster. 'Have you heard that two German spies were arrested in Newcastle?'

'No. When was that then?'

'Oh, last week some time. It was hushed up, of course. They were dressed up as nuns. A bus conductor noticed their hairy arms and reported it to the police. They were followed and were caught red-handed trying to blow up the Tyne Bridge.'

It was exciting stuff and good entertainment as we stood listening to the gossip in the queues at the store grocery department, or in Tommy Maughan's barber's shop. The stories were repeated and improved upon in the schoolyard and one of our pastimes would be the hunting of German spies. One inoffensive old man became our 'suspect' for no other reason than that he carried a small attaché case which Jimmy Durkin and I had decided was a radio transmitter. We followed him on several occasions hoping to catch him sending messages to Germany. But an eccentric old woman, who wore a man's cloth cap and a shawl, became our chief suspect.

Ministry of Information posters declaring: 'EVEN THE WALLS HAVE EARS' and 'CARELESS TALK COSTS LIVES' reinforced these ideas and excited our imagination.

But gullibility had its limits, so when one day I was confronted with the unlikely story that an American Airforce Officer had appeared on Wallsend High Street asking for directions to Carville Road and was later seen entering my front door, I took more than a little convincing.

'Yes, Ginger, it's true. This very important-looking fella, dressed like an Air Marshal, asked his way to your house.'

'You're having me on. I don't believe you!'

But, just the same, I thought I'd better go home. I sauntered nonchalantly, not to show too much enthusiasm, in case they should think I had fallen for their leg-pull.

Imagine my surprise and consternation as I climbed the back-stairs and heard, coming from the kitchen, what I took to be the rich tones of an American accent. I experienced a jumble of emotions – excitement, wonder, fear and intense curiosity. Then, suddenly, I was overcome with shyness and I stood glued to the spot, afraid to make my entrance. Eventually, Kate opened the door: 'What are you doing there? Come in.'

'Yes', shouted Ma, 'Come and meet your Australian cousin'.

Bill Burke was Auntie Maggie's eldest and a fine figure of a man. Not tall, but with a military bearing and extremely handsome. It was obvious that everyone present was immensely proud. Bill had arrived out of the blue – a wonderful surprise. And, out of all the relations, it was fitting that he should arrive on our doorstep for Ma was the only one who had kept regular contact by letter with Auntie Maggie. Nevertheless, there were petty jealousies to be overcome among the aunts for Bill opted to stay with us. This meant that Dave and I gave up our bed to sleep on the floor, but we would willingly have slept on burning coals, so proud were we of our Australian Flying Officer cousin. I looked forward to walking by his side, basking in reflected glory, on Wallsend High Street.

It is strange, however, when I recall that there were other conflicting sentiments which slightly troubled me. It is even more strange that, having been formed in a Catholic home and educated in the Catholic system, on a diet of Catechism, Gospel and devotions to saints, we could emerge, not with a strong conviction that the poor were indeed blessed, but rather with a feeling of shame because of our poverty. I pondered what our well-to-do cousin would think of our cracked lino floor, the very basic furniture, patched bed linen and a general atmosphere of frugality in spite of Ma's efforts. But, thank God, Cousin Bill had no qualms – he wallowed in the jumble of working-class domesticity. He also revelled in a round of parties in every home of the McGuire clan.

BROKEN ARM

Over the next two or three years Cousin Bill made several visits to Wallsend and every time he stayed with us. It was on one such occasion that an incident occurred that was to influence my leaving school and entering the adult world rather prematurely. Jimmy Durkin and I had been serving at the altar for Benediction one Thursday evening. Afterwards, in no hurry to go home – or anywhere else for that matter – we dallied around the church and school buildings looking for a diversion. We found one. I spied through the keyhole of an outer door in the infants' school. There I observed a meeting in progress – the Women's Legion of Mary. They were the devout women of the parish and, as was their practice at the beginning of their meeting, were kneeling in a circle reciting the rosary. It was Jimmy's turn to take a peep. As he bent down to look through the keyhole, I quickly opened the door, pushed him inside and pulled the door close while he struggled to open it. I was helpless with laughter while Cousin Jim fumed with rage, and when he did break loose murder was in his heart. He chased me down the road but because of my mirth I was no match for his speed. I stopped suddenly to let him run past. He grabbed me and, falling backwards, he pulled me down on top of himself. Unfortunately, in the tangled heap of limbs and torsos my right arm was heard to crack, and the intense pain caused me to let out a piercing scream which brought passers-by running to my assistance. By chance, one of them just happened to be my Australian cousin, Bill Burke. He took me to the hospital where I was patched up and strapped. I recall a particularly painful and sleepless night with my worried Ma in attendance. Within a day or two I was out of pain, but I had the excuse I needed. There were three months' compulsory schooling to go before I could legitimately take my leave and look for a job in the shipyard. I now made the most of the facts. I was incapacitated and that was that. It was goodbye. Goodbye to Sandy McNulty, and goodbye to Jingling Joe. Thus I left school at thirteen years of age.

LAND FIT FOR HEROES

The year was 1945. It will not go down in history as the year Ginger McMullen slipped the leash and left school prematurely, but it is remembered as the year hostilities ceased. The end of the war in Europe, V.E. Day, was celebrated in every city, town and village. Every church, school, street and household in the land gave way to an explosion of mirth and merriment. Young and old sang and danced in public places. Mountains of savouries, scones and apple pies appeared on trestle tables in every street to delight the children. Pianos were wheeled into gardens and even on to highways. And beer flowed in rivers. Many soldiers, sailors and airmen came home to celebrate and were given the freedom of every binge in their locality. An atmosphere of good humour and goodwill swept the nation, and it lasted for several weeks.

In Diamond Street, where I was the ever present gatecrasher, the party began with a splash of formality. Everybody was seated and one or two self-appointed toastmasters in turn made a victory speech, but the contribution that lives on in my memory was made by the man who had to be pressed into saying a few words, Tom Potter. He had been for some years a Prisoner-of-War in Germany. After his release, he hurried home to his wife and children and arrived just in time for the street party. He was given a hero's welcome and was our guest of honour. After much persuasion, Tom eventually stood up and made the briefest of speeches.

'All I have to say is, that I hope this is the last bloody Victory party we shall have to celebrate for the rest of our lives.' A moment of sobering silence, and then he sat down to applause. Everybody sang, 'For He's a Jolly Good Fellow', and then we all dived into the most enormous blow-out imaginable.

That evening, and for several to follow, bonfires lit up the night sky, and a tour of each in turn became a popular pastime. This was a new experience for the younger children, for the wartime blackout restrictions had not permitted the traditional Guy Fawkes celebrations to take place. But, in any case, this was different. Instead of fireworks,

End of War Street party

there was community singing around the bonfire, often to the accompaniment of an accordion. The effigy that was cremated was not that of Guy Fawkes but of Adolf Hitler.

As the euphoria subsided in the weeks that followed, it seemed to give way to an atmosphere of tranquility and, in spite of the rationing and austerity that still continued, everywhere there was a feeling of hope. This was a new beginning.

In the post-war years of full employment it was easy to find a job. Young people were introduced to the adult world with ease. It was almost a natural progression from classroom to shop, workshop or office. Most fourteen-year-old lads in Wallsend were absorbed into the shipyard, and some into the mines. Others might find their way on to building sites, which seemed to mushroom on the outskirts of every town, for a massive building programme of council houses was started to herald the 'land fit for heroes and live in'.

As for me, I stumbled across a job and drifted into employment without having given a moment's thought to prospects or career. I did not know, or very much care, where I was going or what I wanted to do with my life. One thought dominated, 'I must work, I must not be lazy like my Da'.

Looking back, I can see that there was a lack of direction, counselling or guidance, but I was no more aware of that than most of my acquaintances would have been of any similar lack in their lives. We were working-class, and we knew our place. There were hardly any role models who had aspired to, and achieved, higher things. And, if they had, you may be sure that they would have been put down with 'who does he think he is?'. Of course there was the notable exception of Albert Stubbins,a shy man and the Newcastle United and England centre forward, who lived around the corner and who would be approached almost daily by the children of the neighbourhood to pat him on the back and say, 'Good owld Bertie'.

When my fourteenth birthday arrived, though the summer term had not quite ended, I knew that I could legally take a job. It was a warm July day. I was sauntering, going nowhere in particular, when I spotted Jeff Allinson at the top of a long extension ladder. He was wearing white overalls and he was painting.

'Hello Jeff.'

'Hello Ginger.'

'Can you see the river from up there?'

'Yes, and I can see the Jarrow ferry.'

'I didn't know you were a painter.'

Jeff came down with ease and skill carrying the paint pot and brush in one hand and casually sliding the other hand down the side of the ladder. With an air of importance he explained how new apprentices were only allowed to scrape and sandpaper and sometimes to apply undercoat if they were skilled enough.

'But look at me,' he said, leaning back slightly and closing his eyes as he spoke. 'I'm doing the gloss.'

I knew he was boasting because Jeff was like that, but I was still impressed. He didn't seem like a lad any more. He talked like a man, and when he took a packet of Woodbines from his pocket and nonchalantly lit up I was won.

'Do you smoke?' he said, offering the packet.

'No.' As soon as I had replied I wished that I'd said, 'Yes'.

'This is the trade to be in. Everything needs to be painted, shops and offices and with all the new houses being built there'll be stacks of work and plenty of money. I get fifteen bob a week already and I've only been working since Easter. Better than the shipyards.'

'I bet you would like a job here, eh?'

'Er ... yes, I think I would.'

'Shall I put a word in for you? The boss will be here soon.'

'O.K. Shall I wait?'

I was soon to realise why Jeff was so keen to recruit me. Every small firm of builders and decorators and plumbers in those days required a horse – the two-legged variety – to push the wheelbarrow. Up to my arrival on the scene Jeff had been the horse. Now it was me.

At eight o'clock every morning I set off with a carefully stacked barrow containing ladders, step ladders, brooms, pots of paint, brushes and buckets, wending my way through the traffic in Wallsend High Street and on to who knows where. Sometimes it was thankfully a short journey with no hills but all too often it would be a few miles journey at the start and finish of every day. Traffic, of course, was much lighter than it is now. There were few private cars. Vans and lorries were also thin on the ground, but horses and carts were still much in evidence. Double-decker buses were my chief concern as I weaved my way pushing a thirty-foot extension ladder with all its accoutrements along the narrow streets of Wallsend and the surrounding area. I did not like it. The embarrassment of being seen by my peers, especially the girls, was so painful that it kept me awake at night.

I did not know how to effect my escape, but things came to a head on a memorable occasion when the boss, his assistant and Jeff loaded the barrow, sent me on my way and then took the bus to Benwell where a butcher's shop awaited the attentions of the master decorators, a distance of eight miles. Could I ever forget that journey? Negotiating the busy streets of Newcastle city centre was a nightmare, and straining every muscle to push the heavy load up Westgate Hill was too painful for words. In fact I might never have made it were it not for a generous middle-aged man, so obviously wearing his demob suit, who came to my assistance and we pushed and puffed together.

'How far have you come with this load?
'From Wallsend.'
'From where? You're kidding!'
'No, and I am going to Benwell.'
'And where are the rest of the gang?'
'Oh, they got the bus.'

He pulled the barrow to a halt, sat on one shaft and told me to sit on the other. He looked at me with fatherly concern. I was touched by his generosity.

'Listen, bonny lad, you don't do that. Not anymore. There's no war, there's plenty of work, and we've got a Labour government. Those days are over forever. Go and tell the bastards to shove their barrow, paint, ladders and their job up their arse, and find yourself something better.'

It took some doing. I rehearsed my lines for the remainder of the journey, and I trembled with anticipation. But I did it, and what a feeling of liberation followed! My pulse-rate was up, and I was breathless for some time afterwards. All the way home I felt a tingle of excitement throughout my body. I strolled into the kitchen to tell my Ma with my head held high, shoulders back and a bit of a swagger. I knew I was growing up.